Sari,

May God grant you the desires of your heart in Him

My Child
WAKE UP

Copyright © 2019 by Charlene Coutet

All rights reserved. No part of this book may be reproduced in any form without permission in writing from the copyright owner.

Unless otherwise stated all scripture references are taken from the New King James Version®. Copyright © 1982 by Thomas Nelson. Used by permission. All rights reserved.

Some scripture references are taken from the following versions:

The Holy Bible, New International Version®, NIV® Copyright © 1973, 1978, 1984, 2011 by Biblica, Inc.™ Used by permission. All rights reserved worldwide.

The Contemporary English Version, (CEV) Copyright © 1991, 1992, 1995 by American Bible Society. Used by Permission.

The ESV® Bible (The Holy Bible, English Standard Version®), copyright © 2001 by Crossway, a publishing ministry of Good News Publishers. Used by permission. All rights reserved."

The 21st Century King James Version®, copyright © 1994. Used by permission of Deuel Enterprises, Inc., Gary, SD 57237. All rights reserved.

My Child Wake Up

Printed in the U.K. by Advent Press Ltd.

Edited by Tamara Muroiwa & Karin Dusabe
Cover Design by Ashley Bloom
Design and layout by Kenneth Rivera
Sanctuary illustrations by Ashley Bloom

For my Sister and sisters:
Taneisha, Zippora, Kia & Cassandra

Thank you for all the love, advice & support throughout the writing of this book.

Contents

1	The Mistake	10
2	The Dream Part 1	19
3	The Plan	29
4	His Entrance	34

Restoration Zone 1

5	The Courtyard & Door	36
6	Holding On	44
7	The Altar	51
8	Changing Him	58
9	The Laver	66

Restoration Zone 2

10	The Holy Place	71

11	The Candlestick	76
12	Going Deeper	88
13	The Table of Showbread	93
14	Talking Longer	99
15	The Altar of Incense	109
16	The Veil	122
17	Where is God?	130

Restoration Zone 3

18	The Most Holy Place	141
19	What is Love?	154
20	Submission Saved The World	165
21	The Dream Part 2	179
22	Epilogue	187

Foreword

Among the many long lost treasures of scripture is the Jewish Sanctuary or Tabernacle. Entrenched in the oft considered monotonous pages of Exodus, Leviticus, & Deuteronomy, the sanctuary remains overlooked, under-studied, and seldom applied. The rich theological insights from its structure, services, and place in the Jewish economy would color eternity with hues of hallelujahs even if only partially grasped.

Yet, we do not find any vigor for its study, especially among youth. It seems to be relegated to a table discussion for theologians, pastors and arm-chair theologians who debate the meanings of hooks, nobs, oil mixtures, and various versions of the structure throughout Israelite history. Before all these modern day, end-time considerations, the apostle Paul, the greatest teacher outside of Jesus Himself, made a staggering application. You are the temple of the Holy Spirit. You are the sanctuary of the Spirit. The church community and the individual believer.

In other words, Paul made it personal. All those laws, rules, instructions delineated in the OT, that seem so pedantic and perfunctory, are actually quite personal. They embody God's belief in the sacredness of you. The sacredness of your body. The implications of such a truth extend their tendrils into the far reaches of our lives. Within the same textual context of Paul's application of the sanctuary to the soul, Paul presents the most pressing implication for the church in Corinth: sexuality, the sin against our own bodies.

So many young men & women today carry a past checkered with abuse, manipulation, and uncomfortable boundary crossing. There is never a justification for inappropriate behavior without consent. Nevertheless, emotional hurt resulting from incorrect information, ignorance, or an easily defeated resolve is preventable. The pages that follow prove this very fact. As we journey through the experience of "Our girl" I imagine many will resonate with her struggles, her journal entries, her biases, her steps and missteps, and hopefully her eventual deliverance.

Char accomplishes some enormous things simultaneously throughout this book. First, she confronts the myriad of assumptions that undergird boundary crossing and a failure to act as if the body and soul is sacred. Secondly, she breaks these assumptions down with simplicity and without theologically dense language. Thirdly, she corrects them with a Christ-like gentleness and leads the reader into a Christ-centered conclusion. Finally, she quietly wins your heart over to the beauty of the Jewish sanctuary and its message to us today.

I cannot fathom a scenario in which any honest young man or young woman, raised with values inside a Christian family, could read too far without marking the bottom of the page with a hashtag: me too. My prayer for anyone reading this volume is that when you get to the end of the journey with "our girl" you'll be able to find healing, clarity, and liberty from past mistakes as well as a new found flame to protect the sacredness of you. Marking the last page of hope with the hashtag: me too.

- **Sebastien Braxton**

Preface

"Wake up."

"Not tonight Lord, not again. Please; I'm tired."

"My child, you need to wake up."

"But I'm so tired; it's 3am!"

"It's time to wake up. We need to deal with your guilt. We are going to get you to move on from your hurt so I can bless you with a brighter future. Wake up. It's time to let go. This has gone on too long; your delay is causing you pain. It's hindering the plans I have for you. I want to fix it for you. Wake up."

"Okay, okay...I'm up. But we've been here before and I still haven't made it past this!"

"This time is going to be different, my child. This time I am going to show you how."

That was 3am on a Wednesday morning for the girl of our story. It was the last of a week-long series of "wake up calls," each at the same time. No matter how late she went to bed, the call still came clearly at 3am. It seemed God had had enough of her procrastinating over her personal issues, and each night had woken her up to "fix" one. You see, Our Girl was very good at identifying, yet ignoring her problems. She would recognize something she needed to deal with, realize how much it would take to face up to it and let go, and swiftly resort to burying it in the depths of her mind, to deal with "later". Of course, she never did deal with it later; she had become an expert at avoiding the issue, locking it up while convincing herself that everything was fine. That she'd get around to it later. Secretly hoping that over time it would simply heal itself; that she would eventually forget about it.

She never did forget, how could she?
It never healed itself, why would it?

This book is a window into Our Girl's experience. An experience through which she finally confronted her fears and became free from the emotional burdens that had weighed her down for so long. Our Girl found joy and peace in that early morning wake up call, a healing and direction that could only come from the One who has a plan and purpose for every life. It is the writer's hope that whether using life's distractions to cover a past too painful to ignore, whether searching for answers to deep relationship problems, or whether simply curious to follow her story, every reader may gain something from these pages that will bless their walk with God, and their communion with others.

1 | The Mistake

Our Girl and That Boy were having an argument. She had thought they were all good; they'd been talking more, and had grown to know each other better. But inevitably the dramas came back. Not about his going out to nightclubs, but other stuff she would later not even fully remember.

"You know what, maybe we should end it here. For good this time," he retorted.

"I've told you, I'm sorry! I wasn't even thinking about the going out thing, you know! You brought it up. I called you back to apologize, didn't I? I came over to say I'm sorry."

"Yeah, to go for a walk, walk and talk. So here we are, walking and talking. You know what your problem is? It's like every time I come near you, you think you're gonna get pregnant and I haven't even touched you!"

Our Girl stopped, astonished. She felt like she'd been found out. With a reputation as the prude of the century, deep down that was exactly what she'd thought. What with everything she'd heard about his previous relationships, she was constantly afraid he would try to do something she wasn't comfortable with. Afraid, because she wasn't sure she'd be able to say no.

"You're wrong," she squirmed.
"I'm wrong?"
"I'm just shy." In her surprise, and overwhelmed with a sense of guilt, Our Girl tried to find shelter in the lie. But rather than that being the end of the matter, covering her feeling of shame, her words only led to the much-feared enquiry,

"So if I touched you, you wouldn't get scared?"

Her stomach clenched in fear and uncertainty. She'd never expected to find herself here, and she was rendered speechless; heart racing, completely unprepared. Wasn't being with a church boy supposed to protect her from this kind of situation?

In her panic, she couldn't see this was probably the most important answer she'd ever been asked to give. Her mind was a complete blank. After so many compromises, all the good advice she'd ever received seemed too far away to grasp hold of. She had kept God, and everyone else, out of this relationship, convinced she could do it all on her own… and now when she needed an answer she felt she had nowhere to turn, and no God to call upon. She felt alone and afraid.

Her heart cried out, 'Of course I'd be scared, it's wrong!' But habit took over. So used to following her emotions, Our Girl was incapable of doing anything that might upset him. The truth was of course, she was afraid – terrified. She didn't want to be touched like that – she'd been brought up to know right from wrong, and this definitely wasn't right. Not wanting to face breaking up with him again, unable to find the words to answer his question, she simply shook her head.

Knowing right from wrong is no guarantee that when the time comes we will make the right choice. Our Girl hadn't taken the time to really know what she stood for and why. Going with the flow, holding opinions without giving them any real thought, had left her void of conviction when an answer was required, speechless and helpless. Her lasting thought was if only she had been able to stand up for what she believed in, things could have all turned out so differently. If only she had taken the time to learn the 'why's behind all of the 'no's she had been taught whilst growing up.

The lie gave That Boy his cue.

So he touched her, and kissed her in a way she didn't know a kiss could be. It was deep, strong and full of desire. Her body awakened in a manner unknown to her. That touch, that kiss, took her breath away, and with it what little guard she had left.

Our Girl was confused, so out of her depth she had no idea what to do. 'Is this my body?' she thought. Absorbed in the rush of emotions, she barely thought anything of his hand moving to her leg and then up and around her body, exploring all over. She was caught up in being kissed, and his touch just intensified the feeling. He carried on for a few minutes, and then stopped.

She blinked a few times in shock and he smiled at her. Her mind racing, she thought to herself, 'Okay, well I'm not pregnant!' Her thoughts were clouded by the whirlwind of emotions, the intensity of feeling in her body, and she told herself that being touched didn't seem all that bad. She reasoned that the kiss had felt so right it couldn't possibly be wrong. Well-practised in allowing her feelings to lead her thinking, she had no way of stopping those emotions from taking over yet again. Common sense, and rational thinking, had no place to operate.

Reflection

> "If I say, "My foot slips," Your mercy, O Lord, will hold me up. In the multitude of my anxieties within me, Your comforts delight my soul."
> Psalm 94:18-19

The enemy is on a mission to derail and cause us to slip up in any way he can. He pushes and pushes, demanding our entire allegiance and he will not stop to let us catch our breath. He knows that if we have a single moment to breathe, the door will open for us to hear the Holy Spirit, for reason to kick in, and we will see the foolishness of what we are getting into.

There is a saying, "It never rains, but it pours." In a downpour, no one wants to get caught without an umbrella; if you had to go outside you'd be mad not to take one. That umbrella can be seen as a symbol of God's all-sheltering love. All Our Girl had to do was reach out in that moment and claim the promise in the verse above, and the help she needed would have been there. The strength to tell the truth would have been hers. Jesus' promise to anyone who calls Him is, "He shall call upon Me, and I will answer him; I will be with him in trouble; I will deliver him and honor him" Psalms 91:15.

This deliverance is promised to everyone. Even if you are not going through trials at this moment, we all face problems at some point along life's journey, and how much better to be equipped with the tools to overcome now! Knowing the why behind the "no, that's not right" is the only way we can build our resolve in the right way. By taking the time to do this we can be ready with an answer when temptation comes. Learn the promises that God has given of deliverance and strength in times of trouble. Repeat them constantly; fix them in your heart. Don't wait like Our Girl, searching for the tools only when it's already too late.

Her problem, however, went beyond lack of courage in the all-important moment. Afterwards, when That Boy was kissing her, it felt like he loved her. But the love he was expressing was very different from what God had intended her to experience. That Boy was presenting the enemy's version of love. Satan tries to bypass God's love, offering us an emotionally-driven alternative. He keeps us so wrapped up in our feelings that we miss the real deal.

Romantic boundaries can seem old-fashioned, out of touch with reality. As Our Girl later found out, these principles are not outdated at all, but are there for good reason. Marriage is a legal contract whereby two people mutually give themselves to each other. They have made a binding agreement, through which each now belongs to the other. With that come rights, an exclusive prerogative to treat and be treated by one's spouse in a way distinct to any other person.

If we blur this distinction, interacting with others in ways that fall under the marriage privilege, we damage our future relationship with the person with whom we do eventually make that agreement. The purpose of exclusivity is to allow a deep and real intimacy, so we can know another human being profoundly, through a shared and private experience. No matter how well we know the person we are with, no matter how special the relationship, that belonging, that mutual ownership, comes only with marriage. We say we are 'given' and 'taken' in marriage. But how can we give or take if we've already given and taken that which sets marriage apart from friendship? That separation must be kept, or the marriage vow makes no sense!

Activity outside marriage that triggers a sexual response puts us in a position conflicting with the essence of marriage. God gave the gift of intimacy to marriage alone because He knows that outside of that, it soon takes over, killing off all means of real communication. Without a serious commitment to God and each other, our feelings quickly supersede our ability to maintain healthy relationships. We stop genuinely talking to the person we are with, ending up with no mutual interests. The relationship becomes based on sex alone, with none of the other elements of what a relationship should be. The result? Eventually the relationship dies, with both parties grown apart.

We can see this in the parable of the wise and foolish builders found in Matthew 7:24-26:
"Therefore whoever hears these sayings of Mine, and does them, I will liken him to a wise man who built his house on the rock: and the rain descended, the floods came, and the winds blew and beat on that house; and it did not fall, for it was founded on the rock.

But everyone who hears these sayings of Mine, and does not do them, will be like a foolish man who built his house on the sand: and the rain descended, the floods came, and the winds blew and beat on that house; and it fell. And great was its fall."(KJV).

We are to build our lives and relationships on the Rock that is Jesus; He is our only firm foundation. If we build our relationships on Jesus and the principles He teaches, we will be able to withstand the storms of life and our relationships will remain intact. However, if we build our lives and relationships on physical intimacy, society, music or bad habits, we are building on sand. When the storms of life come, how will we be able to stand? Our house will fall, and 'great will be its fall'.

If you have had sexual experiences outside of marriage, can you identify with this? Being truly honest, did you feel entirely content, guilt free or complete? Was the relationship a fulfilling and uplifting experience? If you were to remove the sexual element, would that relationship be resting on a firm foundation? Did you feel secure?

Don't fall into the trap, however, of thinking God is a killjoy out to take the fun out of relationships. Marriage and intimacy are gifts from Him; He is the one who said, "It is not good for man to be alone." He is the one who created a wife for Adam. The enemy would have us think God is keeping all the fun stuff back from us, that He is miserable and out of touch.

This is nonsense. Sex only exists because God created it – just like laughter, smiles, giggles or hugs. Do you think the Creator of the most beautiful, interactive experiences of love and enjoyment could be a miserable, boring being? God - contrary to what Satan leads us to believe - is the most fun Person in the universe. Simple, wonderful joys of life such as smiling, kissing, holding hands, sharing a meal, being tickled, laughing until you can't breathe, loving someone and being loved back all come directly from Him. He designed sex as a fulfilling expression of love between a mutually committed man and woman.

However, if these beautiful things from God are used at the wrong time or in the wrong way, pain is the usual result. Laughing is a wonderful thing; laughing at someone else's expense is hurtful and destructive. Food is a delight given by the Creator; eating wrong things or without self-control, although 'satisfying' in the short-term, leads to discomfort and disease. An intimate sexual relationship without binding commitment might in many ways appear to be a wonderful relationship, but is it the experience God intended? Is there not something missing? Where is the sense of security? What happens if it doesn't last?

Are our relationships reaching the full potential of what God intended?

Often they don't, and we are left unsatisfied. God-given gifts cannot survive long when separated from Him. They change into something else in the attempt to maintain the feeling; a quick fix. Sexual intimacy in a relationship that has shut God out almost always depends on lust for its fuel and preservation. This traps us, and we lose the sense of contented freedom. Sexual expressions become one-sided instead of inclusive, driven by self-gratification, which actually drives those involved further apart.

That Boy had no regard for the things that were important to Our Girl, like her personal privacy or purity. He was trying to demonstrate love through behavior that has a 'right time,' set out by a wise, loving God. Their relationship didn't fulfil the conditions to justify such behavior, but his life choices had made it seem 'normal'. It was not normal for Our Girl. But the two were oblivious to their fundamental differences. Apparently, this was what people in love were supposed to do. A pivotal misunderstanding.

2 | The Dream Part 1

"Wake up..."

"Not tonight Lord, not again...please! I'm tired."

"My child, you need to wake up..."

"But I am so tired and it's 3am!"

"It's time to wake up; we are going to deal with your guilt. We are going to get you to move on from your past hurts so that I can bless you with a brighter future. Wake up; it's time to let go. It has been too long and your delay is causing you pain and is hindering the plans I have for you. I want to fix that now. Wake up please."

"Okay, okay, I'm up...but we've been here before and I still haven't made it past this!"

"This time will be different, my child, and I am going to show you how."

So Our Girl woke up properly and lay there quietly waiting, just like she had done the other nights. It was then that she saw what looked like a room, with dark wooden walls and a light-colored floor. There were very few objects in that room; they included a table with chairs and something you could describe as a fireplace. A girl was in the room and

THE DREAM PART 1

the door was open. She was alone, and she was standing looking at the door with her arms wrapped around her body, looking like she was waiting for something. She braced herself against the draft that was coming into the room from the open door. The breeze was cold and the fire appeared to be doing nothing to warm her. She continued to stand and wait. She looked lonely, and a little bored.

Suddenly a man with big dirty boots walked in through the open door and the girl's face lit up. All at once she didn't notice the cold and instead was absorbed with the male in front of her. She found him fascinating! As she welcomed him, he began to walk around the room. He walked around the room with those boots and began to leave horrid footprints all over the light-colored floor. But for some reason, although the girl could see the dirt, she didn't seem to mind; his being there meant she was no longer alone. She busied herself attending to his needs, set a place at the table for him and placed a loaf of bread on his plate.

At first she tried to clean the floor as he walked about the place, and she discovered that the mud came off easily enough to begin with. But soon it began to dry, and it became so hard to clean the floor that eventually the girl stopped cleaning and just left her visitor to keep walking. As she continued to watch, the girl was struck with how disrespectful this man was! He was big, burly and unshaven, with dirty clothes and no manners. He just walked around like he owned that room and eventually sat and ate of the bread that the girl had laid out for him till he was full, whilst providing little useful company. Still the girl didn't seem to mind. After he had finished eating, he stood up from the table and stomped right out of the room, leaving the girl alone once more. He didn't close the door behind him, and once again she began to hug herself against the cold draft. This poor girl was more miserable than before and even worse off because now her lovely light-colored floor was covered in caked-on mud. She tried to clean it, but her efforts got her nowhere and after working for what seemed like an age, she looked up and saw she had barely even made a start. So she sat back in despair and gave up. After all, what was the point in continuing when the mud was so dried on? Instead, the girl opened another cupboard and pulled out a rug that covered a good part of the dirty floor so it couldn't be seen all that much anymore. She straightened out the rug just in time, because no sooner had she finished than in walked another guy through the open door. Once again, her face lit up.

Soon she was busy tending to the new guy, and everything seemed to be fine. The only problem was this guy also had boots on. At first he was happy to keep his feet to the already-dirty areas, but soon he began trampling over her nice new rug as well! To Our Girl, it seemed like this guy did talk more than the other guy, but nonetheless, he was still not the best of company. Eventually he too sat down and had his fill of the bread that was there. Then, just like the other guy, he got up and walked right out of the door without looking back. He, too, left the door wide open and the cold draught seemed to be worse than ever. The fire in the room may as well have been an ornament for the heat this girl could feel from it. Again she hugged herself in despair and stood waiting, looking at the door and lamenting over her even dirtier floor and her ruined rug. She didn't even bother to try to clean it, figuring any attempt to do so was bound to be as futile as her previous effort.

She soon began to cry desperately over her situation

and the cold that she was experiencing until she heard a knock at the door. This seemed to puzzle the girl because nobody had knocked before. As the door was open, they only had to walk in. She turned around to see who it was and there stood a man in pristine white garments, holding a red bucket in his hands with the words, "Precious Blood spilt for you", engraved on the side. It was clear from her face that the girl wanted nothing to do with the strange man at the door and instead turned her back to him and continued to cry. The knocking continued and eventually the girl turned back around to face the man. He said to her, "Let Me in."

After Our Girl had seen all of this, the room disappeared from her view and she heard God say to her,
"My child, this is your story and you are not alone. There are countless others who have been trying to make it through life with the exact same pain, disappointment and guilt. I want you to go to them and share with them what I am showing you tonight. Share it all."

Again Our Girl saw the room, the girl and the floor. God continued,

"That room is your heart, and that girl is you and every other person who is trying desperately to fill their heart with love. Your heart is the center of your body and your body is a temple, and in that temple only true worship to Me should occur. Your body contains the same parts contained in the sanctuary in Heaven.

This is the same sanctuary I gave plans to Moses and the children of Israel for, to build for Me in the desert. Each part of the Sanctuary is ordered; only those people chosen and ordained by Me can enter each place, and only at the time appointed to them.

Those people who walk through your sanctuary with no respect are like squatters who not only have no home of their own, but no respect for the home that you have. That home is your heart. These people have no regard or understanding for the roles they are to play in your life. They have no idea who they are or where they should be. These are they who run through life following paths of their own choosing, and are essentially lost and wandering. They treat your body like a public house rather than a temple. They traipse into your life with all of the mud and dirt of their own wanderings and mistakes. They eat of the most sacred things in your house, and once they have taken their fill and want no more, they leave, not even closing the door behind them. All they leave is an empty, dirty space and a draught.

These people can have all the appearances of being good company, and sure enough they do stop that feeling of loneliness for a while. But for how long? The loneliness that you are feeling is not due to lack of a partner in your life. **It is a lack of Me!**

You have not allowed Me into your life and that emptiness can never go away unless you come to Me. Only I can fill you, my child, and I have promised to fill you. Do not be fooled by the actions of those who have the appearance of doing right. You must test their hearts. For a time they will avoid all the wrong things - just like the second man you saw avoided that girl's rug for a time. My child, you must understand that a mere show of consideration is no guarantee of true affection. Time would have shown you these things but you have rushed in too soon. Be still and know that I am God; wait on Me and I will show you the way. All I ask is that you look for My directions and to purpose in your heart to do what I say, even if you don't understand. All will show itself clearly in good time. Have patience.

You know you have a problem of avoiding your problems. Why? Does it make them go away? That girl's floor was still dirty underneath her new rug in the same way that your temple – your heart – is still dirty, even though you try to mask your pain, guilt and despair with fancy clothes, jewelry, makeup and the appearance of living a righteous life. You cover yourself up and put on such a facade that you are hardly even recognizable and yet, My child, you want everyone around you to see you for who you really are! Who are you?

Do you even know?"

The Lord continued,

"Hiding behind these things which have no power to save or to cover is futile. Sooner or later, you will be exposed and you will have to face that guilt. Why not choose to face it now, before circumstances force you to? Having a dirty floor is no incentive to live a life of cleanliness and purity, but you are deceiving yourself if you think that you can continue to survive without facing your guilt and pain. Regardless of the things you have done and regardless of the things that have been done to you, you are my child and I love you and will heal you, if you will let Me in and stop running. I will forgive your sin and heal your guilt. I will take away your pain. My child, you have carried these things for too long. Give them to Me.

It is entirely your decision. You have the choice to allow Me in and to close the door...or you can leave it open. But by leaving it open you place yourself at the mercy of others. To anyone passing by, the open door is a clear sign that the room of your heart is a public house and is open for business. My child, can you see that this doesn't apply only to relationships, but to any temptation to sin you encounter? Temptation will **always** come, but is it not better to force it to knock at a closed door, than allowing it to walk freely into your life?

My child, listen very carefully to Me now. That floor is the foundation of your heart; it is the foundation of your sanctuary and this represents **purity**. By allowing these people into your life without due regard you have allowed them to defile your Most Holy Place. You have given to them the showbread that was to be before My face at all times, and you have given up many of your most precious possessions as a human person. And to what end?

What do you have to show for your efforts at finding love and loving in return? Only an empty and defiled temple with an open door, dirty floor and an awful draught. I know that you are cold and lonely; I can see that you are sorry for what you have done. Do you not know that I made you beautiful and that you are worth so much more than this?"

As Our Girl continued listening, a passage of Scripture she had known all her life came to her:

"Or do you not know that your body is the temple of the Holy Spirit who is in you, whom you have from God, and you are not your own? For you were bought at a price; therefore glorify God in your body and in your spirit, which are God's."

THE DREAM PART 1

(1 Corinthians 6:19, NKJV)

God carried on,

"You are mine. I have given up everything for you. I knew that you would turn away, but I still came. I still died. I still paid the price for you with My life. Why? I came because I love you. I came because I love you with an everlasting love and I want you to be with Me always.

Will you let Me into your heart?

I will clean you up and strengthen you to study My word. In My Word, I have given clear guidance on how to stay clean forever. Allow Me in and I will close the door and will give you the strength to keep it closed. The door needs to be closed so I can be alone with you for a time so I can begin the clean up process. If you do not allow Me to close the door, you are leaving yourself open for yet more guilt and even more pain... it will not stop.

How long do you want all of these cycles of mistakes to continue?

Give Me this time with you and you will not be disappointed. If you follow the guidelines outlined in the sanctuary I gave to Moses, you will remain whole forever. I promise. My child, I have called you to be a sanctuary – just for Me! I want you to learn and remember the following things and repeat them to yourself always:

> 1. Your body is a temple to the one true God, and it was made for true worship. Worship is the only thing authorized to take place in this temple.

2. Those who approach you must do so with respect for you and reverence for Me and must know where they can and cannot go: they must know their role.

3. You are the temple-keeper and must set the rules – based on My guidelines – and make them clear at all times.

4. You are not a public house; you are My child and I love you always."

That was the offer to Our Girl; the same offer God wants to make to all. There was her way out. That night, for the first time in a long time, things made sense and she understood what had happened. She was so tired of struggling under the weight of her guilt; she knew she had done wrong and strayed far from God. Over the years after her breakup with That Boy, Our Girl had become painfully aware that secrets are poisonous and she had become sick of her own existence. After this revelation, she lay there contemplating the choice between her current path, or making a break with her current way of life and taking up God's offer.

It was now clear that the reason she had failed was because she was trying to fix things herself and solve her own problems. Every time she came out of one of her "expeditions to find peace," she realized she had found nothing of the sort, only more disappointment.

Here was an offer for everything to be done for her. God said that He would close the door and clean up the mess that had been made. All Our Girl had to do was to let Him in. "How on earth do I do that?" she thought. How is it that she found it so easy to let in the rubbish, but found it such a big deal to let in the Good? She had no idea what to do. She went back in her mind to the image of the girl in that room, and yes: that girl's face was an exact picture of her own despair. It was then that Our Girl said, "I don't want to be miserable anymore God: let's do this..."

3 | The Plan

Many see the Sanctuary as an Old Testament relic; as a thing useful for worship in the past, but, since Calvary, no longer serving any purpose in worship today. It makes sense in some ways because we don't have to bring animals for sacrifice, our ministers don't wear special garments on the same scale, and we are no longer required to worship in a specific geographic location. How then is the Sanctuary still relevant to our worship today? More importantly, how is the Sanctuary relevant to me, and my relationships now?

From what Our Girl was shown that night, the Sanctuary is most certainly relevant to our lives today, more than we possibly even realize. I would hazard to say that after the cross, the Sanctuary is the most practical tool we have been given to shape and guide our lives.

The Sanctuary or Tabernacle was the center of the Israelite social economy and the entire setup of their society revolved around its services. God gave the Israelites the pattern of the Sanctuary as a place for Him to dwell among them, and so they could have a tangible model for their worship. It served as a very visual and practical way for the Israelites to draw closer to their Creator and Redeemer. These same principles apply to us today.

1 Peter 2:9 says, "But you are a chosen generation, a royal priesthood, a holy nation, His own special people, that you may proclaim the praises of Him who called you out of

darkness into His marvelous light" (NKJV).

How wonderful to be "chosen" of God! He has chosen us to be His vessels of praise; we have been built for worship. But how does all this talk of worship play a part in my relationships? Well, worship is all about relationship. Worship is an act of giving your time, love and attention to someone or something. There is the idea of interaction, the giving from one and the receiving by the other. That giving and receiving is a basic definition of relationship. Our lives, when conducted as God intends, are to be the tangible, visual and practical demonstration of the saving love of Christ to the World. Our relationship with God will be seen by others in the way we live our lives. It is this primary relationship that will determine the quality of all our other relationships, especially the relationship with our spouse or future spouse. The Sanctuary message has never been more relevant than now, when the world and its relationships are in darkness and in desperate need of that "marvelous light" that comes from knowing God.

"What? Know ye not that your body is the temple of the Holy Ghost which is in you, which ye have of God, and ye are not your own? For ye are bought with a price: therefore glorify God in your body, and in your spirit, which are God's." (1 Corinthians 6:19-20 KJV)

This passage has such attitude in the KJV and I love it! Paul begins the sentence with, "What?" as a means of conveying the idea that what he is about to say is definitely something we should know and that if we don't, he's about to tell us! He writes that our bodies are to be a temple, a place where God's Spirit can dwell. This was the exact purpose of the Sanctuary back in Old Testament times. God wanted to come and dwell with man. How incredible that this was the same passage of scripture God revealed to Our Girl in her dream!

Paul goes on to say that we have been bought with a price, and so should give glory to God in how we operate our bodies and our attitude because these belong to God. The level of ownership God claims over us is shown marvelously in this passage. We don't belong to ourselves; we haven't been left to our own devices to figure life out on our own. No, we have been redeemed by Christ and given a second chance, and with that chance God has given us an owner's manual of how to conduct both ourselves and our relationships, telling us our body is a temple of God. We can drastically improve the trajectory and outcomes of all our relationships if we model them according to the pattern God has shown us though the Sanctuary.

The pattern of the wilderness Sanctuary was given to guide Israel in how acceptable worship should occur, so that God's Presence could dwell with them. 1 Corinthians 6:19-20 shows us that God has the same intentions for our lives now as He did back when He gave the Sanctuary pattern to Moses. So it would makes senses for us to have counterparts of the same features that made the Old Testament Sanctuary acceptable for God's holy presence to dwell in. The Sanctuary was where God came and spoke to His people; it was where He gave them instruction and it was where His plan of salvation was demonstrated. It was a pretty big deal!

The layout of the Sanctuary was precisely ordered; everything had its specific place and function. The layout of the structure consisted of three areas. First was the courtyard: this then led into the Holy Place, and the final area was the Most Holy Place. The three areas each served a specific purpose and were a collective representation of the plan of salvation, laid out by God for each one of us. In the following chapters we will take a closer look at these three areas of the Sanctuary and the various objects found in each part. We will jump back into the story of Our Girl, seeing the smaller mistakes she made in the lead up to that big mistake shared earlier. As we follow her experience, we will consider how she could have gone about things according to the Sanctuary model we have been given by God. We will learn about the Sanctuary service, including who was allowed to be in which place and at what time, and take a look at the roles each article in the Sanctuary was meant to play in her life and in ours. We will see just how complete and practical God's plan is for our relationships, and how we can be built up if necessary and heal from past mistakes, as we step through the Sanctuary door and advance right up to the Most Holy Place and the Presence of God.

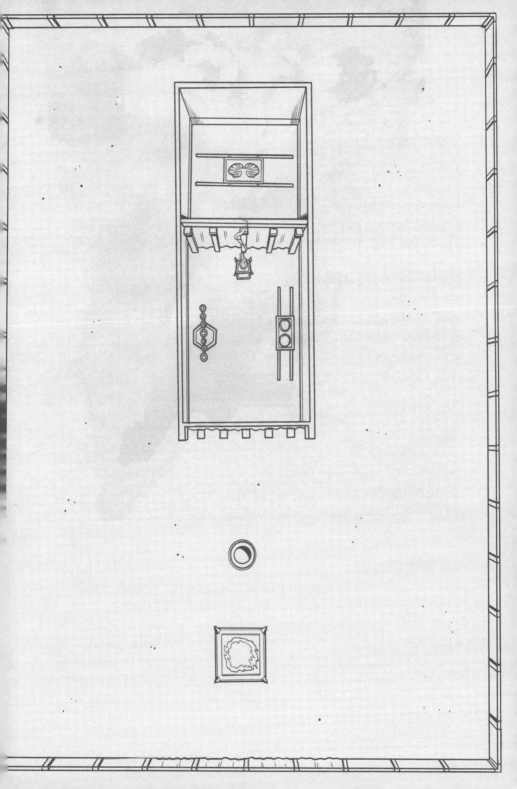

4 | His Entrance

Mistake Number 1 - Judging Others

He walked over and was introduced to her by a friend.

"Is this him?" she thought.

After all this time and having heard so much about him, the person in front of her just didn't seem enough. He was nothing especially out of the ordinary and certainly didn't seem like he was able to fit the part she had formed for him to play in her mind. From what she had been told, the reality of him just didn't seem to fit: he was just a regular boy!

Her mistake was not that she thought he was a regular boy when in fact he was secretly a superhero. Her mistake was rather forming an opinion purely from the opinions of someone else.

That first encounter and subsequent interaction took her guard down, and in getting to know That Boy, she thought she had him all figured out. In her mind she was being so clever in finding out he was 'different' to the things she had been told, and she thought herself so 'Christ-like' in her acceptance of him. Little did she know that although in many ways he was different to the opinions everyone had of him, there was still a great deal of truth in the warnings that she had been given.

How did things turn out so badly when she was so sure she knew what she was doing? How is it that something as basic as misjudging someone based on others' opinions could go on to so drastically shape and change her life? After all, she was a grown woman, or so she thought. In her mind, she had it all figured out. As far as she was concerned, her philosophy was, 'No matter what life throws at me, I will always do the right thing.' She thought, she was so 'advanced in wisdom' and had such a thorough knowledge of God that she really thought she was progressing in godliness by getting over her initial prejudices and becoming friends with this boy. It was only later that she realized this was in fact mistake number one. By judging him by the standards of her own mind rather than by God's standards, she unwittingly set herself up for what followed as her guard came down.

So That Boy made his entrance into Our Girl's life; she let him in and got to know him. They would see each other from time to time and she slowly began to see what all the 'fuss' was about. You see, he was so incredibly charming! He had a way of carrying himself, a way of looking at people and a way of saying all the right things. He was so very likeable, and she began to like him. The feelings were small and insignificant for a while; so much so Our Girl didn't even realize they were there. But because she had allowed him to enter into her life and had begun to spend time with him, she had opened up her heart to what he stood for and what he was about. She didn't feel the need to guard against those small initial feelings because they were 'just friends'...right?

5 | The Courtyard & Door

Restoration Zone 1

The courtyard is symbolic of the space in our lives where we admit the people we wish to become closely acquainted with, i.e. the friendship zone. This was the area of Our Girl's life into which That Boy made his entrance. The first point of approach to the Sanctuary was to bring an acceptable sacrifice to the door of the courtyard, which was on the south side of the tabernacle. Upon arrival the worshipper was met by the priests, who would carry out the sacrifice. The person bringing the sacrifice would then lay their hands on the sacrificial emblems to be offered, and the offering would be accepted and taken to make atonement for their sins.

The problem of sin is that it separates us from God; part of the reason for the Sanctuary service was to show Israel how God had planned for them (and indeed all humankind) to be reconciled to Himself. Sin naturally leads to death. As such, God had to find a way to save us from it in a way that would prevent its continuing on for eternity. This bringing of a sacrifice by someone who had sinned was a very practical and visual way for God to teach His people the results of sin, which was death. It also demonstrated that through a substitute, or sacrifice, we can instead receive the gift of forgiveness and life.

The sacrifice brought was to be a voluntary offering,

given freely by the individual seeking forgiveness and a closer experience with God. The practice was a symbolic representation of the greater sacrifice of Christ, that would ultimately cover all our sins once and for all. The Sanctuary was a constant reminder to the Israelites of their need of a Saviour, and helped them understand more fully the process that the true Lamb would have to go through.

So to gain admittance to the Courtyard of the Sanctuary you had to come with the purpose of reconciliation, or a desire to draw closer to God. So too for us today in a practical sense. This area of our lives serves the purpose of admitting those who are not merely general acquaintances, but rather have a purpose and desire to draw closer to us and to God. These people will not just be listed as our friends on social media; rather, they will have our direct phone numbers and are the people we see often and spend regular time with.

The first interesting point to note is that the only way into the sanctuary was through the courtyard door on the south side. Jesus said, *"I am the way, the truth, and the life. No one comes to the Father except through Me."* (John 14:6, NKJV). Likewise for us, Christ should be the only way and standard by which someone can gain access to our temple courtyard. All of our closer acquaintances should be considered in relation to Christ's character and the life that He led. The people who are aiming for this standard of Christ in their lives, or who display these characteristics if they're non-believers, are the ones we should surround ourselves with the most. Having these people in our closer spheres will allow them to provide solid spiritual support and influence us for good. The characteristics we should look for are listed in Galations 5:22-23: "love, joy, peace, long-suffering, kindness, goodness, faithfulness, gentleness, self-control."

Our Girl did not have Christ as the standard by which people could enter her "courtyard". She allowed people in simply based on whether she thought they were interesting, or whether she felt a liking or attraction for them, which is precisely how That Boy was able to enter her life and close circle of friends.

Do the friends we've surrounded ourselves with now display the standards of Christ in their lives, or are they more interested in doing things their own way? Do they have a genuine level of respect for you, or do they gossip to others and bring gossip to you? What type offering do they bring to your life?

The entrance of the Tabernacle was where a person came and essentially laid himself or herself bare before the priest who was ministering there. The individual showed their sincerity and devotion to God by bringing an offering that was "without blemish or spot." Essentially, it was the best offering they were able to give and was as perfect as possible.

In the same way, we first of all need to consider whether we ourselves are bringing our best before God. Are we really coming before Him in all honesty, knowing that He is the only One who can fix us? Or do we act more like Cain, bringing what we think is acceptable and hoping that God will acknowledge it anyway? Cain brought what he believed God ought to have accepted. So when God did not accept his offering, he got angry and ended up killing his brother Abel; Abel's sacrifice was acceptable to God, and this was something Cain could not take.

So often we take exactly the same course as Cain, bringing before God our idea of what He should accept. Our offerings of friendships and relationships are very often made up of things we have put our own hand towards creating, so we feel deserving of acknowledgment for our efforts and get angry when God doesn't shower us with praise.

Do we desire in our relationships to really give of our best, do our best and have Christ as our standard? Or do we approach others in a way whereby we bring what we want to the door of *their* sanctuaries, with no consideration for the requirements set up by God for a correct offering? When we offer our love to others, is it the best we have? Is it acceptable to God?

Approaching the Sanctuary was to be an act of worship because that place was holy, set apart by God as a dwelling place for His presence. However, approaching a person does not mean you are to worship them! We are to pursue relationships with others with an understanding of and respect for the fact that this person is a temple of the Holy Spirit. Strange as this may seem, it does not matter if we think the person has God in their lives or not. The very existence of that person means they are a sanctuary made by our Creator, regardless of whether or not they are operating their bodies and minds with that understanding. The priests and Pharisees in Jesus' day had turned the temple into a place of commerce and business rather than honoring it as a place of worship, but did that stop the temple from being the temple? No indeed! The requirement for reverence and true worship remained, as stated by Christ when he overturned the tables of money. Quoting Isaiah, He said, *"It is written, 'My house shall be called a house of prayer,' but you have made it a 'den of thieves.'* " (Matthew 21:13).

Our focus text asks, *"Do you not know that your body is the temple of the Holy Spirit?"* (emphasis supplied). The text does not say our bodies 'could be' a temple as long as we do this or that and behave in such and such a way... No! Instead it clearly says that each of us is a temple *regardless*, which means our bodies should be treated as such. Our bodies are literally places of worship!

The people we have allowed into our circle of friends will clearly show who they have as their standard by the way they speak, the things they like to do and the places they like to go. But of all of those things, the things we talk about and how we say them are the clearest indicators of where our hearts are aligned. Jesus Himself said, *"...out of the abundance of the heart the mouth speaks."* (Matthew 12:34,). If all that comes out of our mouths is negative towards self and others, then that is the condition of our hearts! Christ in speaking to His disciples explained that it is not the things that go into the mouth that defiles a person, but rather the things that come out of a person, in thought, word and deed. Do our thoughts, words and deeds cause us to defile others and ourselves? Here is a very serious text that raises the stakes:

"Do you not know that you are the temple of God and that the Spirit of God dwells in you? If anyone defiles the temple of God, God will destroy him. For the temple of God is holy, which temple you are." (1 Corinthians 3:16-17.)

God clearly takes our respect for self and interaction with others very, very seriously – with significant consequences for those who fail to uphold His standard for the care and wellbeing of their own temples and others'.

The importance of good friendships cannot be stressed enough; it has been said that "we are known by the company that we keep".

- Our friends are a true indication of the standards we aspire to live by.

None of us desires to be alone or amongst people who have vastly differing values to ours, but whether we acknowledge it or not, we all crave community. So if we find ourselves constantly seeking the fellowship of people who have denied God, above those who are seriously seeking him in a genuine way, what is that saying about the values of our hearts? If we naturally gravitate towards the company of the opposite sex and seek as much intimacy as we can find in relationships outside of marriage, what does that display about our character and desires? However favorable our intentions may be in any of these scenarios, God knows the reality of what is in each of our hearts, and we only deceive ourselves if we think the company that we keep does not show clearly the condition of our hearts.

"Your associates may not be expected to be free from imperfections or sin. But in choosing your friends, you should place your standard as high as possible. <u>The tone of your morals is estimated by the associates you choose.</u> <u>You should avoid contracting an intimate friendship</u> with those whose example you would not choose to imitate..." *Our High Calling* p.256.

I think, of all the points we will look at within the Sanctuary, this first checkpoint of the courtyard door is the most important.

If we lower our standards of entry then we allow many of the wrong people into our lives, many of whom are the very ones to bring us pain and drama. These people's influence ends up influencing our values and habits. It is from this group of individuals that we choose who to enter into dating relationships with, from whom we eventually choose our spouse. Is it any wonder that so many of us end up with horrible relationship experiences when we haven't upheld Christ as the standard of entry? Is it any surprise that there are so many of us lamenting that we can't seem to find the right spouse? Maybe he or she hasn't been allowed entry because of the self-made standards at our doors. Or maybe we have not been allowed entry into their lives, because our standards don't meet up with those they have allowed God to put in place there. So often we miss out on each other, on relationships God purposed for us to have, because we haven't taken adequate time with God to establish things according to His ideal.

All too often we forget that every person on this earth is a child of God, and His treasured possession; that we ought to show to them the same respect we wish to show Christ, and have Christ as the standard of entry to our own hearts.

If you truly want to change the path of your life and relationships, take time in your Courtyard. Take the time to truly set up Christlike standards of entry into you closest sphere of life. Not everyone could come into the Courtyard in Israel, only those seeking reconciliation with God. The rest of Israel and humanity were outside in the general community.

However, sacrifice was the characteristic requirement of those who sought entry to the Sanctuary. The thing about bringing a sacrifice is it requires you to realize you have done something wrong, and need to let go of your sin. If we never take the time to self-evaluate and recognize our need of God, there will rarely, if ever, come a time where we feel the need to make a change and seek reconciliation. We will never think we need to let go of anything, or deny ourself things. This was exactly the situation of Our Girl.

6 | Holding On

Mistake Number 2- Denying The Reality Of The Situation

This time round, Our Girl's mistake was the result of continued naïveté. She just didn't take the time to see things for what they were. She was too busy enjoying the feeling of the unchartered territory of the situation – a kind of excited playfulness – and didn't stop to engage any sense of rational thought about what was actually going on. For many people, analyzing situations like that is considered boring, right? Our Girl had convinced herself that thinking things through too much would 'kill the mood' or 'deaden the magic' of the moment. If she had really engaged her brain, all the things she knew to stay away from would have immediately come to mind, and she would have had to keep away. The problem was she didn't *want* to keep away; she wanted to go further! She wanted to feel all the things she was beginning to feel, to be the apple of That Boy's eye: she wanted him to look at her and smile in the way she had seen him do to others. She wanted to be close to him, because in him she saw something she didn't think she could ever have herself, something so enticing...

That something was 'freedom' – a bewitching sense of freedom without concern or conscience.

My Child Wake Up

Our Girl was in complete denial of the reality of her involvement with That Boy and was holding on with no desire to give him up. Most of us would agree that being dishonest with ourselves does not help us in the long term. The short-term gain is a whole lot of feelings and emotions that the carnal part of us really enjoys at the time...but because they are based on a lie, the long-term result is a painful wake-up to harsh realities, which often result in emptiness and loneliness. Our Girl didn't know the future results of her decision to leave her head behind in this adventure. She simply would not sacrifice That Boy. She had always been accused of thinking too much about things and reading too much into situations. This time, she decided to be 'original' and let her heart lead for once. She never got the memo that heart without brain is just as bad as brain without heart. Both lead to mistakes, pain and emptiness. Lying to herself about the reality of what That Boy was becoming to her meant she was, in fact, trying to hide things from her own conscience, if that were even possible! Not facing the facts meant she would go on to become something she was never supposed to become. But she wanted this so badly! She wanted an escape from the apparent boredom of her own life, and a fast-track one-way ticket into the supposed excitement of his. She wanted so many things, without knowing what it was she really needed.

Well it so happened that Our Girl fell deeply in love with That Boy, and he became her everything. Everything – that was the problem. He triggered so many new desires that she didn't even know she had in her. She was blinded by this 'freedom' and so intoxicated by the thrill of this VIP entry to a carefree life, that very soon she couldn't function without him.

45

In her mind, they were both so similar. She wanted to live a life which would add excitement to her disciplined and ordered upbringing, while he was already living a life of excitement and secretly wanted to bring some order and purpose to his own. 'The perfect combination,' Our Girl thought. She figured that she could help him with the parts of his life that needed fixing, and in return she wanted him to fix the boredom and monotony of her own, and to love her. The problem was they were both seeking something they needed or wanted in the other: it was **in** each other they expected to find the missing part of their lives. Because of that, they both failed.

The following is an excerpt from a diary entry Our Girl wrote at the time:

> "We both got on so well and after like a week or two, I was closer to him than I had ever been to anyone. We saw each other for the next five weeks every weekend and things were perfect. We were just amazing friends first and foremost but with that extra bit on top. Things were slow and steady, no rush of emotions that needed constant fuelling. Sometimes yeah there was that overwhelming need to be together when we were apart because just sitting in each other's company was so fulfilling and left me with a complete feeling I'd never felt before. Well we talked all the time by text during the day and by phone in the evenings and we were so close. He told me things about himself that he's only ever told his best friend before and that's how we were."

Things between them began so well and that feeling was

addictive – literally, just like a narcotic. She was so content in what she thought was the simplicity of everything: only later did she discover the depth of that illusion. Things were only simple because she wanted them to be. The enemy of souls certainly has a way of getting us to feel comfortable in places we shouldn't be. Consider how Our Girl found her sense of completion and contentment in That Boy. He became the answer to her questions in life, he was all she wanted because of how she felt around him.

She would later discover – the hard way – that there is no person on earth who can give someone true contentment in life. Moreover, true contentment cannot be found if your life is separate from God.

Her diary continues:

> *"We had so much in common and he fulfilled all my expectations except for one vital thing on my ticklist and that was religious conviction. He just wasn't that interested or enthusiastic about it but at first it was ok because he knew this and was changing for himself. So he was cutting down on his going out to clubs and was focusing more and everything was great. He treated me so well and was always aware of me when I was there but we weren't obsessive about each other and I never felt neglected even when he was playing computer games with the guys. However I knew that I would have to keep a check on this issue because God is the most important factor in my life and if God isn't at the centre of a relationship, then that relationship isn't going anywhere and will never last."*

You can see clearly that Our Girl was completely convinced God was the most important factor in her life. She was too blind to see that God was only important to her *because she had been taught that He should be* and that it was 'the right thing' to believe in God and be a Christian.

Let us take note of something seriously important. God is not a 'thing' we inherit from our parents. Christianity isn't simply 'the right way to go' because 'that's the rule'. God is infinitely more than this, on every imaginable level and beyond.

Consider the difference between someone telling us a rose smells nice and actually smelling the rose for ourselves. God isn't Someone we can figure out from what another person has said. We have to take that crucial step of actual faith to try Him and find Him out for ourselves, to the point where He actually becomes a real Person to us in our daily experience. Otherwise, He's just some idea we think is handy for a tight spot in life.

To Our Girl, that's who God was: a 'theory'. She had never allowed Him into her life properly. Instead, she let this charming Boy in and used him to fill her up and make her feel loved. It meant she no longer noticed the empty feelings she had within herself, which had threatened to consume her thinking. *'This Boy is the perfect remedy to my emptiness,'* she thought. The reality? He was just a distraction: those feelings of emptiness were still there, just covered over with a pretty dusting of sugar that masked their bitter taste. This is exactly what Our Girl finally saw, when God showed her the girl in the room early that morning. She had known a relationship without God on *both* sides would fail, but her love for that boy was too much. Instead, she chose to hope he would change. In fact, she secretly hoped that she could change him. In any case, there was no way she was going to give him up and accept living without him.

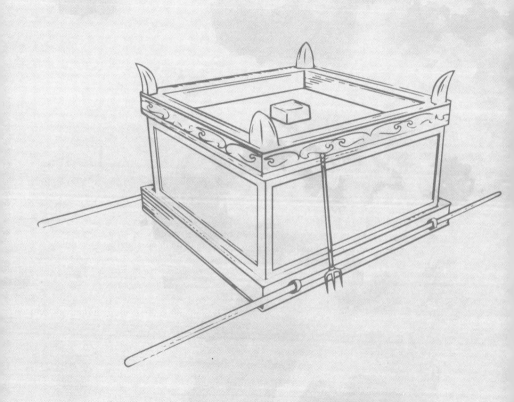

7 | The Altar

The story is told that a beautiful statue once stood in the marketplace of an Italian city. It was the statue of a Greek slave girl. It represented the slave as tidy and well-dressed. A ragged, uncombed little street child, coming across the statue as she played one day, stopped and stared at it in admiration. She was captivated by it. She gazed long and lovingly. Moved by a sudden impulse, she went away and washed her face and found a way to comb her hair. Another day she stopped again before the statue and admired it, and had a new idea. The next day her tattered clothes were washed and mended. Each time she looked at the statue she found something in its beauties to admire and copy, until she was a transformed child. By beholding we become changed.

That is an oft-repeated phrase based on 2 Corinthians 3:18, "*By beholding we are changed.*" So what is being changed in our lives through the influence of our friends and the company we keep? What are we burning on our altars of burnt sacrifice? Are the negative aspects of our characters being 'burnt' away, given up to God? Are we allowing the un-Christlike character defects we desperately need to remove from our lives to be consumed in surrender to Him? Or are we holding on to things we don't want to give up, like Our Girl was with That Boy? By keeping him in her life, she slowly began sacrificing things she should have been zealous to hold onto, instead of the other way round.

Things like honestly, integrity, purity.

If we are being influenced for good, then the negative aspects of our characters should be offered up on our altar of burnt sacrifice. If things are the reverse, and we are being influenced the wrong way, then it is often our purity, good character and reputation that are being sacrificed instead. Ellen White writes,

> "At the altar of self-sacrifice – the appointed place of meeting between God and the soul – we receive from the hand of God the celestial torch which searches the heart, revealing the need of an abiding Christ."[1]

This celestial torch is the very thing we need in our lives to shed light on the path we are to walk. This torch shows us our true condition and our need of a Savior, but how often are we made aware of this need from our fellowship with our friends? For Our Girl, the interactions she had with That Boy did the opposite, causing her to run away from God through her guilt and shame. We, too, may have all too often been to the altar and sacrificed the wrong things, through being reluctant to break the cycle of influence from the people around us. The altar of self-sacrifice will either produce offerings acceptable to God, like Abel's, or those deplorable like Cain's. What does our fellowship say about us?

"Do not be unequally yoked together with unbelievers. For what fellowship has righteousness with lawlessness? And what communion has light with darkness?" (2 Corinthians 6:14) This text is usually quoted in the context of marriage or courtship relationships, but on this occasion let's consider it in relation to basic friendships as well.

My Child Wake Up

The Greek word for 'unbelievers' in 2 Corinthians 6:14 means 'disbelieving', 'without Christian faith' or 'untrustworthy'. These definitions paint a clear picture as to the state of an "unbeliever's" character. They could be confusing, since there are many decent human beings in this world who do not believe in Christ, so the point deserves elaboration.

There are many of us who are 'unbelievers' right here in the church. Look at Our Girl! She found out she was an 'unbeliever,' even though she was not an entirely bad person. The problem was that her actions were not trustworthy as a true example of what is good, because her motives came from herself and not from God. As a result, her example as a whole was not one those around her could follow to reach a Christ-centered life. This is why we should avoid joining ourselves through dating or marriage to those who do not believe as we do; their influence cannot be trusted to lead to what is good, right and of God. Although we may have friendships with non-Christians that are positive relationships in many ways, we need to be very, very careful in our choice of close friends – that is, those whose advice we take seriously. This is not extreme: the issue of whether or not we secure salvation is what is extreme! The sacrifice on our altars is representative of the sacrifice Christ made in dying on Cavalry's cross for us...which was no small thing!

"...love will be revealed in sacrifice. The plan of redemption was laid in sacrifice, – a sacrifice so broad and deep and high that it is immeasurable. Christ gave all for us, and those who receive Christ will be ready to sacrifice all for the sake of their Redeemer. The thought of His honor and glory will come before anything else."[2]

Many of us find it difficult to understand how we can be

radical representatives for Christ in our friendships and relationships. We find it much easier to compromise in (various) little things, some of which may even appear good. But Proverbs 16:25 says, *"There is a way that seems right to a man, But its end is the way of death"*. Very often it is these little compromises, just like those Our Girl made, which ultimately lead to bigger mistakes down the line, causing much pain and regret.

There is a story about a teenage son who asked his dad if he could have some friends over to watch movies. The father asked what kind of movies they were going to watch, and the son replied that they weren't bad films. Sure, there might be the occasional swearword, one or two sex scenes and perhaps a bit of violence, but... at this the father denied his son's request, explaining that those kinds of films were not suitable. But the son insisted the films were mostly good and nobody would really notice the bad stuff. Thinking about how he could communicate to his son the potential impact of small compromises, the father decided to consent to his request and even promised to make the group some homemade cookies. The son was thrilled at his apparent victory of reasoning and went off to organize the gathering.

When the young people arrived that evening, they headed straight for the kitchen, following the smell of fresh baking. The father was just putting the last batch on a plate to cool and the son introduced his friends. The son asked his father what kind of cookies he had made and the father replied, "Well son, these are really good cookies. I bought the best flour and butter and I got the fanciest chocolate chips and oats I could find and that's what I made them from." The son and his friends excitedly each took one of the treats, but just before they bit into them, the father said, "Hold on a minute, there's just one other thing in these cookies...I added just the tiniest bit of dog poop!" The boys immediately threw down the cookies in shock and disgust. The dad looked at his son and insisted, "But son, they are made from ninety-nine percent the finest ingredients; you won't even notice the poop! What's wrong?" The son looked at his father, completely baffled, while the father continued, "You see son, it really doesn't matter if something is *mostly* good, because just the tiniest bit of bad can ruin the whole thing, can't it? The films that you are going to watch and all the other things you may be planning to do tonight may indeed be mostly good. You think the tiny bit of bad will not make a difference, because it is far outweighed by the good. Yet the reality is the opposite – because that little bit of bad could well become the tiny ingredient that grows until it ruins your entire life. I just wanted you to see that." Taking a tray down from the shelf and holding it out to his son, the father said, "Now here is my original recipe, one hundred percent good cookies that I made first for you and your friends. These are much more appealing, aren't they?"

This is a crazy story but the illustration is sound. The small compromises we allow with our friendships and in our lives will have the power to shape our paths and decisions for eternity. Just as the son in the story thought a little bit of evil was insignificant, many of us do the same. How many little compromises do we ignore because we think the good we do will outweigh them?

We should take the time to properly consider the friendships in our courtyard, because it is from these that we select who to allow admittance to the next area, the Holy Place. As shown in the illustration, the courtyard completely encircles the central part of the Tabernacle. In much the same way, the circle of friends we choose will surround our lives. Enveloping ourselves with godly people will help ensure that the other two areas of our hearts are protected and established for good. On the other hand, if we surround ourselves with negative influences, we will soon see them escalate into serious problems that will permeate our entire sanctuary. Let's review a few details from this first checkpoint, the Altar of Burnt Sacrifice, so that moving forward to the following stages we will have a pool of good people to choose from.

- **Have our friends entered into our lives through the Door, Jesus Christ? Or have they found another way to enter into our affections, (including by stealth)?**
- **What are the things they like doing? Are they things Jesus would like doing too?**
- **Do our friends entertain gossip? Does gossip find an ear with us?**
- **Do our friends encourage us to be mindful that we are all temples of the Holy Spirit, and that as such we need to show each other due respect and loyalty?**
- **What kind of offering do our friends bring into our lives? Do they influence us to sacrifice our negative traits on the altar of self-sacrifice? Or do they encourage us to sacrifice our better selves for short-term pleasure that can only lead to long-term pain?**

Going back to the girl in the room, we must not forget our job is to let Christ in. If we are completely occupied in trying to avoid negative or distracting influences, we will never be able to focus on the job God has assigned to us. Ellen White wrote the following:
"I am instructed to say that in the future great watchfulness

will be needed. There is to be among God's people no spiritual stupidity. Evil spirits are actively engaged in seeking to control the minds of human beings. Men are binding up in bundles, ready to be consumed by the fires of the last days. Those who discard Christ and His righteousness will accept the sophistry that is flooding the world. Christians are to be sober and vigilant, steadfastly resisting their adversary the devil, who is going about as a roaring lion, seeking whom he may devour."[3]

The enemy is always seeking to break our focus; he wants us to take our eyes off the door just long enough for him to sneak uninvited people in, that they might lead us astray. Let us therefore be sober and vigilant in our choice of which friends to admit into our courtyard; of who we let influence the sacrifice upon our altars.

8 | Changing Him

Mistake Number 3 - Thinking You Have the Ability to Change Someone

No person can change another human being. We can't even change ourselves – but we'll come to that later. The things Our Girl wanted to change in That Boy were generally focused around his spirituality. His lifestyle was in many ways not one she approved of, and certainly not one she felt he should have if he was to fit her desire for a 'church' boy. This became her focus above all else. Her problem was, she had already chosen to love this boy, and he didn't quite fit the role. Instead of letting him go and waiting for God to send her a boy who did fit the part, she persisted in telling herself he could eventually learn the lines and play along. She concluded it was him who needed to change; after all, there was no way on earth she was going to the places he went to, or joining in with what she assumed he was doing. Besides, he had been brought up in a Christian home just like her, so she figured it shouldn't be too much of a problem for him to go back to those principles.

Our Girl became a stickler for all things 'good'. At first he seemed interested. He did initially start to change for the better and that was so exciting to her! She took this encouraging start as her license to dive in headfirst and to love him with everything she had. The result being, she now faced the problem of being in love with a boy who didn't exist, in the sense that it was the **potential** in him that she loved.

She loved 'the boy who could be' if he would just do this and change that. But day by day, as her expectations rose higher, and were subsequently trampled, frustration set in. Eventually she began to despair. Why couldn't he just see what was so plainly in front of him? Why couldn't he just accept that some of his habits were a pointless cycle, pursuing happiness in all the wrong places? It was obvious to Our Girl because she had chosen to keep seeing things as she'd been taught. He, however, had chosen to look at life his own way and do things on his own terms instead. That was the root and basis of his 'freedom' - the self-appointed license to make up the rules as he went along.

In his mind, the rules he made were the tools that kept him at liberty. In fact they were the very things that caused him to be chained, blinded to the simple truth that he was not happy. Our Girl desperately wanted to fix that.

Indeed, she realized later that she was actually a lot freer than he was. Her freedom manifested itself in many ways. It was the ability to be outside of the cycles that had so many of her peers trapped. It was the ability to operate in life with a clear conscience and an innocence that made day-to-day living fun. She was free from the kinds of drama that come with certain social environments because she did not go to places where she might succumb to negative peer pressure. This left her able to choose where and how she wanted to enjoy herself. Our Girl was the one who was free and That Boy was in actual fact a slave to popular opinion and lifestyle. But at the time, she was completely oblivious to this simple truth.

The enemy always makes the things of this world seem so enticing and liberating to us. His ways appear easy and simple. All Our Girl could see was the thrill of living life as she wanted it to be; she thought that making up her own rules and living by them would be incredible. Psalm 119:32 says, "*I run in the path of Your commands, for You have set my heart free*"(NIV). The freedom Our Girl sought she would later find in the guidelines God had set out clearly for her in His Word; the freedom to run and the liberty of life without guilt. This freedom, however, would come later. For now, That Boy's way had enticed her: she had bitten the bait and was completely wrapped up in wanting to live life his way in some things, whilst at the same time trying to get him to hold on to the spiritual principles he had been taught as a child. Her desires wanted that freedom she thought his life had but her conscience told her that many of the things he was doing were actually wrong.

Our Girl experienced first-hand that trying to change someone is, without a doubt, the most impossible and frustrating thing ever. She tried everything in her power to show him what she thought was right. She reasoned with him until she had no breath left in her, nor motivation to continue. Talking to him became a huge chore because she had taken upon herself the moral responsibility of changing him for the better. She was driven to succeed because she loved him. She wanted what was best for him, and it hurt that he didn't seem to want anything to do with it. His answer was, "I know what's right; I'm just not ready to do it yet." Often Our Girl would ask when he was going to be ready and he would reply, "Oh, when I'm like in my twenties and thinking about getting married and having children. I'm just not ready now, I like things the way they are."
Does any of this resemble the person you are in a

relationship with or desiring to be in a relationship with? More importantly, does any of this resemble you?

That Boy and Our Girl are great examples of many of us today. It seems to be an inherent part of human nature to want to change another person, whilst resisting any efforts to be changed ourselves, especially if we don't feel ready to change, or simply don't want to. Human nature is a tricky thing; that's why the Word of God says to us, "*Let this mind be in you, which was also in Christ Jesus*" (Philippians 2:5, KJV). If we remain locked in our own natural ways of thinking, we will never be able to see and grasp the things that will help us break the cycle of mistakes and guilt. Instead of looking to be a "Christ-minded" person, Our Girl took on the nature of a Pharisee: always looking at the faults of those around her, and being all too quick to express her opinion and denounce their way of life. Her approach lacked both love and understanding, whilst demanding perfection and flawless love from everyone else.

That Boy was equally-but-differently unwilling to take on the mind of Christ. As a result, they both became trapped in the wrong mindset. If we think about it, we very often do exactly the same in fighting to justify ourselves and our way of thinking. Many of us seek to maintain our freedom of thought by our actions, but instead end up enslaving ourselves to the same thing enslaving everyone else: *self*. And we honestly wonder why we can't break out of the cycle of repetitive mistakes! That Boy was trapped in a lifestyle he thought was enjoyable. He didn't want or feel ready to change while he was young, because to him this was the only way to 'experience life'. Our Girl felt a similar way, having adopted the notion that her youth should be spent with a level of freedom from parental rules and regulations. They both knew that if they changed their thinking they would have to face their consciences and change their lifestyles. Neither of them wanted to change. Despite the issues, they were content to make do with life the way it was. Change was too much effort.

The sad thing is that just like That Boy and Our Girl, we rarely see how great that cost is until it's too late – by then we are fully stocked with shelves and cupboards full of guilt.

Let's be honest. Is much of what we strive for actually worth the time and effort? The future isn't as far away as we think. Although we try to run from it, guilt always catches up with us suddenly, and will keep pace with us through the rest of our lives until we face it. In many ways we could say this book is about honesty; let's choose to be honest and take a good look at things now, *before* the guilt and pain has a chance to take over. Back to Our Girl's story. She wrote in her diary,

> *"Well two and a half months later, I've come to the conclusion that it's over. The promising start ended and well with his going out, he's probably got worse or well has just gone back to how he used to be. This whole tension thing started between us after one episode of him going out and coming home in the early hours of the morning and calling me whilst he was drunk. After that, tension between us started, we began to talk about that one thing all the time… always me trying to get him to see sense and he always saying, "But…" We just weren't getting past this drama…"*

In a short space of time the problems that had developed

in their relationship became too much for That Boy and Our Girl to handle. It all happened so fast and Our Girl's heart was breaking. She hadn't realized how much she had allowed herself to love him, and this kind of love was completely new to her. He had become her everything, and every time he did something she didn't like it hurt her terribly, to the point where she felt her world was caving in. Yet she never once expressed these feelings to him. Why? Because she didn't want to 'ruin' things.

They both found it frustrating, feeling they were so close to being 'right' for each other – but the lifestyle differences wouldn't go away. Our Girl's conscience wouldn't let her continue in the relationship while he persisted in the life he'd chosen. So eventually, she told him they had to say goodbye. She had finally begun to realize things could not work between them, and the only thing holding them together was an indescribable longing to be near each other. Our Girl was heartbroken; but at this point she was in a place she could have recovered from.

It was the most inefficient break-up ever! Our Girl knew in her mind she had to leave, but her heart was not convinced, so she didn't leave willingly. She began to feel sorry for herself and quickly fell back into the pattern of following her feelings. She dismissed what she later knew to have been the Holy Spirit's warnings, and instead let her feelings govern her brain once more. For that short period they were apart, she did everything in her power to convince herself he wasn't so bad. She had become addicted to him and spent endless nights trying to find a get-out clause from her conscience so she could go back. She missed him badly...and they were still talking a lot. Too much. What Our Girl should have done at this point was wash That Boy right out of her life and mind, and fill the void with positive things. The problem was, she had no idea how to go about cleansing her heart and mind of the love she had allowed to develop there.

9 | The Laver

Incredibly, we have here another item from the Sanctuary that fits perfectly with what Our Girl needed. In the Temple courtyard there was a bronze washbasin called the laver. This was where the priests washed their hands and feet at several times: before approaching the altar to offer a burnt sacrifice, after having made the sacrifice, and before entering the Holy Place of the Sanctuary. The washing of the hands and feet was symbolic of purification from actions carried out by their hands, and from paths they had chosen with their feet. **If they did not carry out this part of the temple service, they would die.** The constant washing before and after each sacrifice was a continual reminder to the priests and the onlooking Israelites of the importance of being clean from sin. The routine of cleansing before entering the Holy Place was a reminder of the necessity of being clean before entering the presence of God.

The washbasin was positioned in between the altar of burnt sacrifice and the entrance to the Holy Place, to ensure that any dirt and dust picked up by the Priest whilst ministering in the courtyard could be washed off before he approached the Holy Place entrance. This dirt and dust reminds us that, while we may have offered our sacrifices, seen them accepted and our sins forgiven, even on the way to closer communion with God we can pick up bad habits and make mistakes that need cleansing. So, as we also advance in our study towards the Holy Place, let us consider whether there is still anyone in our acquaintance whom we need to wash out of our lives or be cleansed from. These may even include those who have influenced us for good and provided spiritual encouragement in the past, but for whatever reason now cause us to be distracted from a deeper, closer walk with Jesus. Even closer to home, are there things in our own hearts, plans or desires that we need to wash away? So that nothing stops us entering the Holy Place of our sanctuary experience? The priests would have died if they entered God's presence without washing; so we can see if we neglect to be thorough in our cleansing process, to be serious about our commitment to holiness, we too can face consequences. Jeremiah 2:13 says,

"For My people have committed two evils: They have forsaken Me, the fountain of living waters, And hewn themselves cisterns – broken cisterns that can hold no water."

How many of us have fashioned our own idea of purification? We think as long as we only do X, Y and not Z, we are still okay to carry on without hindrance. How many of us set up our own standards for friendships and relationships, forsaking the example and standard of Christ just like Our Girl did? These ideas, Jeremiah tells us, can hold no water! Jesus cannot abide in our hearts if we hold up our own washbasin of standards. Divine provision has been made for our purity – what a waste if we don't avail ourselves of it!

The constant sacrificing the priests performed daily meant the washbasin was probably the most used item in the whole of the Tabernacle. It was the precursor to every other process in the Courtyard, and the bridge from the

THE LAVER

[handwritten: Christ should be the standard in the sense that he knows/wants what's good for us → we shouldn't anything/anyone less of good into our lives & circles but]

Courtyard to the Holy Place. Christ is the standard we must apply in the choices we make and the paths we choose. Without water the body would die; up to sixty percent of our total bodyweight is water. The human brain, around eighty percent. If we didn't replenish our water store daily, we would slowly wilt and die, just like a plant. Living without Christ in our lives leaves us lacking in the *essential* ethical and moral foundation upon which our sanctuaries are to be built. Every aspect of who we are is completely dependent on Christ to remain functional.

"Unless the spirit and principles which characterized the life of Christ be planted in the heart, they will not control the life. Very many professed Christians are so only in name. They have no root in themselves. They have a superficial knowledge of the truth, and break off some of their evil practices; but the heart is still filled with pride, impurities, unholy ambition, self-importance, and love for the supremacy. The soul temple must be cleansed of its defilement, there must be purity of thought and intensity of desire, united with earnest efforts to meet the standard in God's word, or they will never become elevated, subdued, purified, and wear the white linen which is the righteousness of the saints, and become fitted for the companionship of the pure and holy."[1]   *[handwritten: *stores in doubt*]*

How important this washbasin is! Christ, our fountain of living water, longs to have a real place in the way we conduct our lives. He wants to be the standard of all our choices and decisions. He alone can remove the *"pride, impurities, unholy ambition, self-importance, and love for the supremacy"* from our hearts.

Only Christ can help us to cleanse our friendship circles,

[handwritten at top: the concept of having to meet a standard of "purity" before even being allowed in God's presence doesn't sit right w/ me. That isn't the calling that Jesus made to us.]

My Child Wake Up

but we need to make Him our standard. Imagine being able to see a reflection of your face in the water before you wash your face – just as people did before mirrors were available. Now make a link between that water in the washbasin, which cleanses us, and the work of Jesus Christ.

As we wash our lives in Him daily He will show us our blemishes and everything that needs to be cleansed in our lives. Having a clear view of ourselves isn't much fun, but without these regular checks we will become deluded concerning our real condition, and eventually fail to see our need for purification at all.

Our Girl's mistakes were the direct result of a lack of self-examination in the mirror of Christ. Never did she take the time to look into the bad areas of her life, or to use Christ as her standard for her relationships. She avoided God purposefully – resulting in the deadening of her conscience – so she could carry out her own plans on her own terms. She found it much easier to look at others and find fault with them than to do anything about her own faults. Having Christ as a checkpoint in her courtyard would have eliminated That Boy from her circles right away – and this book would never have needed to be written!

[handwritten in margin: intense doubt]

Our challenge is to constantly remember that it is Christ who leads the purification of our lives. Keeping His standard high will be a clear sign to all that there is no room or entrance for those who will not abide by His code of conduct. Think back to the batch of one hundred percent good cookies the father in our illustration made first. God's standards have been prepared for our good, to bring us fulfillment as we go through life. It is when we compromise with little bits of bad here and there that we find situations coming into our lives which ruin the whole experience. Let's get back to the original plan designed by our Creator and allow our courtyards and friendship circles to be washed and purified by Christ. This way we can have temple courtyards where acceptable sacrifice is willingly made.

10 | The Holy Place

Restoration Zone 2

The Holy Place of the Sanctuary was the 'next level' in the Sanctuary system. Using type and analogy, it expanded the Israelites' understanding of the plan of salvation. Only specific priests and Levites were allowed to go into this area: so it should be also for our sanctuaries. Only those who have been ordained by God should be allowed into this area of our lives. It is not a place for all of our friends as a whole. The Levites were a family specifically chosen and called by God to work together in the upkeep of the Sanctuary and the delivery of its worship services. In the same way, our holy place is where family and intimate friends can be in close proximity, working together for the upkeep and nurturing of our individual selves. Some of us may be the only ones in our family who believe in God, but don't worry! In these situations, the time we have spent really filtering through the people in our courtyards will come into play.

If we have made a consecrated effort to restore things to how they should be in Zone 1, we should easily be able to identify those who are like family and have demonstrated themselves to be trustworthy spiritual associates. The family members we do not feel will be a good support to our spiritual journeys must remain in our courtyards. Not admitting them into our holy places does not mean we disregard them or their position in our lives. Respect is always due! But right now, we are talking about establishing our *spiritual* support system. This sanctuary-restoration process is not one of alienation or separation from responsibility and duty. The fifth commandment is very explicit: *"Honor your father and your mother, that your days may be long upon the land which the LORD your God is giving you."* Exodus 20:12. Having respect for our fathers, mothers and others demonstrates respect for God Himself, for it is God who gave the commandment in the first place.

The spiritual family we admit into our holy place must be those who are fit to perform the duties required of them. Likewise, if we are to be admitted into another person's holy place, we too must understand the responsibilities we are to fulfill there. This line of thinking applies not just to family and close friends, but also to the person we wish to be in a closer relationship with. He or she must demonstrate themselves willing to be a guardian of our sanctuary, not one who will defile it. The Bible asks us, *"For how do you know, O wife, whether you will save your husband? Or how do you know, O husband, whether you will save your wife?"* (1 Corinthians 7:16) There is a great deal of responsibility placed on the spiritual condition of those in marriage relationships. Both need to have a solid spiritual foundation, so that when the time comes that either needs encouragement, both parties are equipped to support each other.

Personal relationships of this kind find their beginning in our courtyard, and gain substance in our holy place. Time spent cultivating our lives in this area is foundational to the way our relationships will continue into the future. This determines whether the relationship will be a success or a miserable failure. The next effort of our study must go into examining the Holy Place worship practices, so that we can know how to order this area of our lives, as well. The standards we develop should be high, but not so high that we ourselves cannot attain to them. We cannot make demands of a person, in terms of their character, if we are not prepared to meet those same demands ourselves. Therefore, much time needs to be spent in constant self-improvement and spiritual development.

There is no point waiting for the 'perfect' person to be with if we ourselves are not taking the time to be the 'perfect' person in return. What a shame to waste our precious time looking for a partner, rather than building our own characters for God's Kingdom! The reality often ends up being like this: our Mr or Mrs Right does eventually surface on the horizon, only to walk right past us because they do not see in us a character consecrated to Christ. In this holy place of our lives we make the effort to be in a love relationship with a perfect God, whose love never fails. It is here that we learn the tools necessary for lasting and deep relationships, that we learn from God how to be dedicated and loving toward an imperfect person, by experiencing His grace and mercy towards us.

The priests who entered the Holy Place were very much aware of their proximity to the Shekinah glory, the Presence of God, just behind the curtain in the Most Holy Place. They knew that to be in the Holy Place was a privilege they were to never take lightly, and so moved about with what can only be termed 'holy fear'. This was not a fear caused by worry; rather, it was an attitude of reverence and self-awareness seen in every step they took and everything they touched within that sacred environment. If we do not feel this in our interaction with God, then something very important is missing from our Christian experience. We need a renewed sense of Who God actually is before we can develop this holy fear in our Christian walk. As we come closer to God, we will become more and more uncomfortable with our own heart condition. But we should **not** be afraid of moments of discomfort on this journey – it is this very sense of inadequacy that drives us to come even closer to Christ, who alone can fill up our lack and draw us into an even more intimate walk with Him.

In the Holy Place there were three principal objects: the Candlestick (or Lampstand), the Table of Showbread, and the Altar of Incense. The following chapters will explore some of the applications we can draw from these objects in the context of restoration and purity in our relationships.

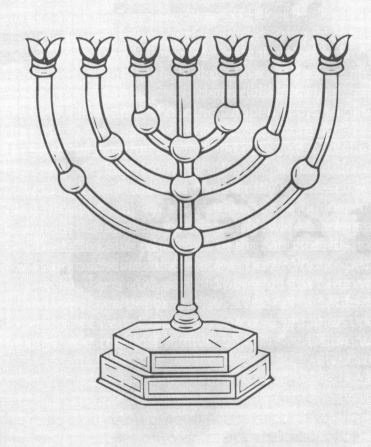

11 | The Candlestick

The Candlestick was made of pure hammered gold and had seven branches – three on either side of a central branch. There were seven lamps on the Candlestick, the oil in which was to burn without ceasing from morning until evening before the Lord. This service of the lamps was to happen continually as a lasting agreement between God and each generation of Israelites. As spiritual Israel, we too can find an application for our lives today.

So what was the purpose of the Candlestick in the Holy Place?

The Holy Place was an enclosed area made entirely of linen curtains protected by a *"curtain of goats' hair, above that a covering of rams' skins dyed red, and over all a covering of badgers' skins, all forming a perfect protection from the weather."*[1] There were no windows in the structure, so one can imagine how dark it would have been inside! It is clear, therefore, that the Candlestick was a very necessary part of the Holy Place setup. Without the light from the lamps it would not have been possible for the priests to carry out any of their duties. So too with us: without the light shining in our lives, everything else we need to do will not be done properly, if at all. This is because we learn to see everything else based on the light we have.

So what is this light? Paul writes:

"But even if our gospel is veiled, it is veiled to those who are perishing, whose minds the god of this age has blinded, who do not believe, lest the light of the gospel of the glory of Christ, who is the image of God, should shine on them." (2 Corinthians 4:3-4)

The light is the Gospel. Simply put, it is the knowledge of Christ's sacrifice on the Cross of Calvary on behalf of sinful man. Paul is here explaining that those who do not understand the truths of the gospel have been blinded through their unbelief by "the god of this age," which could be anything that we put in place of God in our lives. Our blindness is a spiritual inability to see "the light of the gospel of the glory of Christ". Without this light, we are unable to see the truth that Christ came and died for all, giving us all access to eternal life if we believe in Him.

Paul tells us that this light is the gospel message we are to share with others, so that they don't have to live in darkness. In the same way that hiding a lamp under a bowl renders it useless, hiding the Gospel will render its truths useless to others and to us. The unique way the message of salvation works, means it needs to be shared with others before we can fully comprehend and implement in our own lives the very truth we've shared! Hoarding truth, constantly learning without sharing, leaves us full of dead knowledge that will get us nowhere.[2]

This idea makes many of us panic, saying, "I've not learned enough," "I don't understand things fully," or, "there is very little good in my life right now; I can't possibly share anything". It is so easy for us to look at the negative aspects of our lives, to the point where we forget all the good God has already achieved in us. Yes, we may not be where we want to be, but look how far God has brought us! That is something. If we were in a dark corridor and all we had was a tiny stump of a candle, and there was someone nearby with no light of their own, would we not choose to link arms with that person and share our tiny light with them? No matter where we are or what we are doing, we can always share the light that we have, because in this world there will always be someone close by living in complete darkness. Those people are waiting for light, any kind of light, to illuminate their existence.

Our job as light-bearers doesn't necessarily mean we will be present through the entire process of conversion, through someone else's entire journey from darkness to the full light of the Gospel. More often we simply share the little we have, shining the light of truth just a little further than where the person could see before. Sharing the Gospel is a team effort, in which each of us has a unique role to play in the lives of others. Some of us are more often called to spark that initial interest, others are better at following up and nurturing, and still others at gaining a final decision of complete surrender to Christ. Whatever stage we find ourselves at in a person's life, let us share what we have, because for all we know, that may be all the person needs right now. Let's not get ourselves worked up about witnessing; it doesn't have to be that hard! Imagine walking around in the dead of night, trying to hide a lit flashlight under our clothes. The darkness makes it impossible to completely hide the light, because whatever it gets close to begins to glow. It is much harder for us to hide our light in this dark world than it is to share it!

Sometimes, it is as straightforward as telling our own story of how God has impacted our lives personally. Each of our stories is unique, so only we can tell it properly – making every one of us priceless in the Gospel mission field. Our unique set of skills means we each have a unique mission: let's not get caught up looking at someone else's commission and forget our own. Our light is simply the result of Jesus' earthly ministry on our lives.

Our Girl had a serious problem sharing her light with others, and especially with sharing what she thought to be right with That Boy. She was a naturally shy person, and determined that door-to-door or public witnessing was definitely not her thing. She didn't like to invade people's spaces because she didn't like people invading hers. Figuring that by disturbing them she was being rude, she tried to be polite and kept to herself. It was much easier for her to talk about spiritual things if they came up in conversation, but would rarely be the one to instigate a spiritual conversation. Not wanting to be branded as being strange she tended to just keep quiet. Mostly, she was worried she would say something wrong or be asked a question she didn't know the answer to. Being that she had skills in organization and administration, she figured she was one of those 'behind the scenes' people who would keep a low profile and simply ensure everything ran to plan. To Our Girl this was her way of sharing the gospel; this was her area of 'good deeds'. The way she saw it, her services would facilitate others sharing the gospel in an effective and organized environment. Thinking this was her full part in the teamwork of sharing the Gospel, she was very happy with the arrangement; no active sharing, just keeping busy doing things.

The truth of the matter was, Our Girl didn't want to share her story because she was scared her mistakes and insecurities would be found out. She knew deep down that her life was not where it needed to be.

Living under the pressure of trying to keep up appearances can really weigh us down, and put a dimmer switch on our witness. The enemy delights in getting us addicted to having a "form of godliness,"[3] while preventing us grasping the power we can only experience when our lives are truly in line with God. This traps us in the cycle of forever striving to keep up appearances – a cycle that may fool everyone else, but not God.

This was a cycle Our Girl didn't realize she was trapped in. She never really thought she was faking her spirituality, because she really was genuine and entirely sincere in the things she said and did when it came to Christianity. That good church girl she portrayed really was her; but this was only half of who she was, and she desperately wanted that side to be the whole. She knew that the entirety of her person had a darker side, kept well hidden. She desperately wanted to be the carefree, happy, spiritual person most people saw; she wanted to be that girl *all* of the time, not just for some of it. For Our Girl it was the worst possible agony being forced to live however her surroundings required. That was why it took her so long to distance herself from That Boy. He was the only person in the world who she felt she could be her entire self around. She loved that security, as it felt like a haven of peace. Unfortunately, this so-called security was just the result of not having to hide the things she had done from him – because she had done them *with* him. He was the only person she didn't have to keep this secret from. What a subtle setup!

The enemy constantly works in such sly ways that we end

up setting ourselves up to fall time and time again. He drives us to make mistakes, keep them secret and struggle through life trying to avoid being found out, only to seek refuge from the pressure of hiding in the very thing that caused those mistakes in the first place! What a terrible cycle to be enslaved into. To prevent a return to those wrong habits we must find genuine spiritual healing from all the wounds of our past, and reconcile all the different facets of who we really are.

We are back to habits – and we know that habits begin with a choice. The only way we can overcome our bad habits is to allow the Holy Spirit to lead us in forming new ones. These new habits will not be easy at first, but over time as we repeat the same actions, our new, good habits will keep us away from past addictive mistakes. New habits form the bridge to a new us! Letting go is the first step on the road to healing, walking away from who we had become, until we are truly living life as the person God called us to be.

The enemy wants to prevent us from becoming this new person. Even when we form new habits we are not entirely out of danger. Satan's next step will be to persuade us to remain shameful about our negative past, even though it has long since been overcome. He is happy for us to live a more convincing Christian life, as long as we maintain enough shame over our past to keep us from sharing our whole selves with others. He knows that a person who has fully overcome and accepted complete forgiveness through Christ will naturally overflow with joy at their deliverance, and share the story of their victory with all who will listen. Witnessing to others about how Christ has defeated Satan in our lives gives the most convincing evidence that we are victorious in the Gospel. The enemy wants us to keep quiet; he wants to keep people trapped in sin until death, and is loath for us to expose the fact that his plans really can be defeated!

By our silence and reluctance to share our light, we open a door which allows doubt to manifest itself – thus trapping ourselves in a cycle of thinking we are not truly forgiven. We re-live our guilt over and over again, always feeling the need to come to Christ with the same things. Christ longs for us to understand that (in effect) He has no idea what we are continually bringing before Him! He wants us to understand that when He forgave us the first time, He cast the memory of that sin *"into the depths of the sea"*! (Micah 7:19.) God calls to us, saying,

"I, even I, am He who blots out your transgressions for My own sake; And I will not remember your sins." (Isaiah 43:25)

When we come to Christ claiming this promise and ask for forgiveness, we *must* believe that our sins have been blotted out. Our sins are erased; God will not remember them and neither should we, other than to share with others the cleansing power of Christ's forgiveness.

Often those who have the appearance of being good in church whilst living an alternative lifestyle in the week are branded as hypocrites. What the term fails to account for is that there are many who are truly seeking to reconcile two opposing parts of themselves. The war for our allegiance is as serious as war gets, and while many of the battles we have are fought, won or lost in secret, there are those of us whose battles are witnessed in a more public sphere. Instead of branding and labeling such individuals, let us instead empathize and work for the saving of that soul, whose actions are a clear display of the seriousness of the Great Controversy.

This battle for the will cannot last forever. One side will eventually win; either the side desiring the service of God or the one desiring the service and gratification of self. For Our Girl, this reality was evident in her experience, because there came a point where she eventually gave up trying to maintain her level of church existence. She stopped singing, stopped attending Sabbath events and kept herself very separate from most of the church people she knew. This change came about when she no longer had the energy to live both lives effectively. It wasn't because she didn't want to be better – the simple, yet tragic truth was she felt she had no one to help her try, so there was no point going on.

How timely a word of encouragement from her circle of friends would have been! How she would have cherished a heart-to-heart with someone who saw her struggles, and decided to be real with her and share that she was not alone in her dilemma! But once we have overcome our own struggles, we often fail to witness of our triumph, and instead seek the appearance of having been 'holy' our entire lives. Let's be intentional about sharing our past; not by giving glory to the days of self, but rather using our experiences to paint a vivid picture of the saving grace and love of Christ. His is a love that is available to all. Don't those amongst us who are struggling deserve to know that there is a God who really delivers?

And for those of us labeled as 'fronters' or 'hypocrites,' do not stop trying to be in church. Instead, spend time having a serious reality check, because living a double life is draining and unhealthy. The enemy wants to keep us forever running in circles, so he can wear us down until we are fit for nothing. The very fact that some part of our heart feels the need to be in church and to look like we're happy about it is good news! It may feel like an act, because we enjoy being in 'other' places too, but that small desire is evidence that the Holy Spirit is still trying to get through to us. The choice is ours as to which side will win in the end.

For those still under the jurisdiction of spiritual parents, guardians, dorm deans and so on, let's make our decisions for Christ now, while still in that nurturing environment. Convincing us to wait till we can leave and be 'free,' supposedly having the liberty to make our own decisions about church, is just about the biggest trick the enemy has lined up for our downfall. Waiting to make a decision for God and good does us no favors. Rather, it gives us more time to add to our list of mistakes and guilt. If we are struggling to make a decision now, what makes us think we are going to be any better at making it later?

"Today, if only you would hear His voice, "Do not harden your hearts"" (Psalms 95:7, 8). The implication of the word "today" is that we have no idea whether we will be around tomorrow to make the decision. Yesterday is gone and today is all that we have. The world is full of people who have left the church thinking that one day they will come back. The fact that we are able to hear the voice of God today is evidence that we still are in a position to make a change; tomorrow we may find we have become a person entirely incapable of making that spiritual decision.

Perhaps some of us just don't want to let our light shine, and feel the pressure of being committed to something we don't quite 'get,' but which our parents expect us to follow.

As a result we can become focused on the idea of leaving home as our only hope for freedom and happiness. The reality is, once we leave home and begin to exercise that 'freedom' in ways different to how we were brought up, we end up trying to still our conscience, which incessantly tells us that we know better than this. Just like attempting to hide the light from a torch under our clothes in the dark, we end up struggling to hide the light we have in us from our upbringing. We do know better, and it is often very easy to identify a Christian who is trying hard not to be one!

Once we have been shown the best route from one place to another, we will never forget it. Sure, we may choose to take an alternative path of our choosing from time to time, but even as we go down that route, deep down we will always know that there was a shorter path that would have taken much less time and been far easier. Often, the problem we have is not with the route itself, but perhaps we were forced to take it by parents and guardians who may have neglected to incorporate love, humility or consistency in their directions to us. Let us not allow the method of our upbringing to make us think church and Jesus are the issue. Instead, let us see the merits in the path of Christianity, and find a way to walk those well-worn paths with joy when we recognize how liberated we are by doing so.

Perhaps we were made to walk wrong paths in our childhood and encountered experiences that have worn us down, decimated our self-esteem and left us with scars. In such cases it can seem easier to just continue as we have always been. But here the promise is, *"if anyone is in Christ, he is a new creation; old things have passed away; behold, all things have become new"* (2 Corinthians 5:17). It is never too late for any one of us to live free and liberated in the truest sense! God has created us with the incredible ability to learn new pathways of thought and action. Just because we have 'always done things this way' doesn't mean we cannot learn to be different, to live differently or to love differently. We can absolutely learn new and healthy ways of building relationships, where the only dependence is on Christ. By doing this, we will find our earthly relationships will become so much more authentic, fulfilling and safe.

Have you ever wondered why it is written that the *wages of sin is death*? (See Romans 6:23.) Why use the word "wages"? To be able to get a wage a person has to work for it: similarly in this text, Christ is trying to tell us that we have to put in real effort to earn the outcome of death. We have to work really hard to silence our conscience against the light of known truth to prevent that light from telling us that what we are doing is wrong and we have strayed from God. The fact is, we can never entirely silence the truth from our conscience. It will get quieter, and less frequent in its reminder, but it will always be there because truth is truth regardless of whether we believe and acknowledge it or not.

The rest of that verse goes on to say, *"but the gift of God is eternal life in Christ Jesus our Lord."* (Emphasis supplied.) God's way of life is free. We don't have work even a minute to receive it. We simply have to make the choice to accept this promise as truth. There is no time like the present.

> *"For Zion's sake I will not hold My peace,*
> *And for Jerusalem's sake I will not rest,*
> *Until her righteousness goes forth as brightness,*
> *And her salvation as a lamp that burns."*
> Isaiah 62:1

This is the depth of love that God has for each of us.

He will not let any one of us perish without ensuring we have had every possible chance to accept His way out.

Those whom we have chosen to be in our circles of friends and to be closest to us in the holy place of our lives should be encouraging us to seek out truth as it is in Christ and share our light. Let us look to those around us, whom we can see are following God, and ask them what their story is. More often than not, their story will tell of struggles similar to ours, and more importantly, victories that can be ours. Choose today to shine: that better opportunity might never come.

The things Our Girl was brought up to believe were the very things that saved her from her despair, once she came back to them through prayer and a renewed study of God's Word.

Clinging to a God she didn't know, but knew was there, was the best thing Our Girl could have ever done. We should cling tight to Him too, for He will not let us down. Let us clasp him tight with both hands, because using one hand to hold onto our past will only loosen our hold on God. Before Our Girl got back into prayer and studying her Bible she had a number of decisions to make and habits to change. These had a lot to do with how she spent her time.

12 | Going Deeper

Mistake Number 4- Spending too much time together

During the conversations that took place between Our Girl and That Boy after Our Girl had ended their relationship, a seed was planted in her mind. She began to think that all of their problems were actually her fault alone. Whenever they spoke, he was very careful in his choice of words and she was too naïve to see where things were leading. He wanted her back, and she wanted to go back so much that she soon began to regret her decision to leave him. Instead of talking less after breaking up, they spoke even more! He suggested that their break-up didn't really have to be the end of the relationship; rather, it could in fact be a new beginning – a fresh start. After one conversation they concluded that their problems were simply due to not having spent enough time getting to know each other before embarking on a romantic relationship. That not having known each other well enough was the foundation of all their friction and disagreements.

Talking about their problems became the theme of their communication. Never once were any real and direct questions asked or responsibilities admitted on either side. They clearly missed each other, and wanted to be back together. At the same time, it was equally clear that each blamed the other, but was unprepared to come out and just say so. So they talked and talked, each secretly hoping that the other would see it was their fault. With all that time in conversation, Our Girl eventually forgot the real reason why they had broken up in the first place. They seemed to be getting on fine while talking on the phone, and suddenly her decision to end the relationship began to look silly. As time went on, the memory of her pain and frustrations faded, and soon all those reasons that were so clear at the time had faded from view. Her next diary entry, from a couple of months after their 'break-up,' showed a marked u-turn from her earlier conviction. As a result of time in continued close communication, Our Girl had shifted from knowing she had to leave That Boy because of their differences, to thinking she had gotten it all wrong and made a terrible mistake:

"I felt so much more for him which is always the case. You only realize the true value of something when you lose it. He is such a special person who has so much to offer and through all of this issue, he was open and blunt, he told me exactly how he was and all he did was to ask me to accept him and to support him. But the way we were then and more importantly, the way I was then, meant that acceptance and understanding weren't a part of my vocabulary and the stubbornness of both of us in not wanting to change, meant that we weren't going anywhere... I've learned that sometimes all a person needs is a hand to hold and a heart to understand. And that's all he needed from me and me in my stubborn blindness I couldn't do that. I know now that if you want something enough or if you care about something enough, then you should do everything you can to prevent yourself from losing that thing, even if it means changing

and doing something you aren't used to doing..."

This change of opinion was subtle; it came as a result of Our Girl beginning to see the flaws in her own character. She clearly manifested sincere remorse for her previous pharisaism and self-righteousness. She began to look back over her relationship with That Boy, and every time she remembered admonishing him to do better and to change, she applied a little more guilt to herself. Soon enough, that guilt turned into a whole stack of regrets. If only she had been more understanding, things might have been different and they could still be together. Had she been less nagging and less obsessed with what she felt to be 'right,' then perhaps he would have felt able to talk to her and to share his feelings more easily. All these thoughts came to her, as she looked back with eyes fresh in the discovery that That Boy wasn't all to blame, but rather she was to blame too.

But there was a major problem. Not once did she consider the possibility that her principles were in fact correct, that it was simply her *application* of those principles that was misplaced. She was right to acknowledge her own part in the problems their relationship suffered. However, she failed to get her head around the fact that those failings did not invalidate her reasons for ending the relationship. It is an important lesson to learn. Realizing we share blame in a situation does not suddenly make the whole situation entirely our fault. In this context, blaming ourselves completely is as unbalanced as totally blaming the other person. In getting us to switch our thinking around like this, the enemy succeeds in muddying the waters; we become confused in our understanding of right and wrong. As a result, we group good and bad decisions together, throwing out some good stuff we really needed to keep, along with the trash we were getting rid of in our attempt to fix things ourselves.

The mistake of still spending so much time with That Boy also meant Our Girl had increasingly less time – or desire – to communicate with God or those friends and family members who could have advised her. Not spending that time with God also meant she still lacked the tools she needed to overcome her ties to That Boy. Spending time is bonding.

We can ask ourselves a few questions to try and be aware of the issues in this area. Questions such as, "Who are we spending most of our time with?" *"What are they giving us in return for that time? Is it good or bad? Is it just a boost to our feelings or something more enduring?" "Does this time spent together help us face the problems and issues of life? Does it strengthen our character?" "What time of day – or night – are we having these interactions? For how long?" "Is it hard to end the conversation? In that moment when we sign off, does our sense of joy and completion disconnect too?"*

This scenario with Our Girl is a classic trick used by the enemy to get us to return to situations we had already gained victory over. For a moment Our Girl's mind and desire to do right won over: long enough for her to see she had to let That Boy go. But this clarity didn't last, because she didn't walk away from the situation. The time she continued spending with him confused and clouded her judgment, leading her once again to give way to her feelings. This proved to be the foundation for the bigger mistakes she made later on.

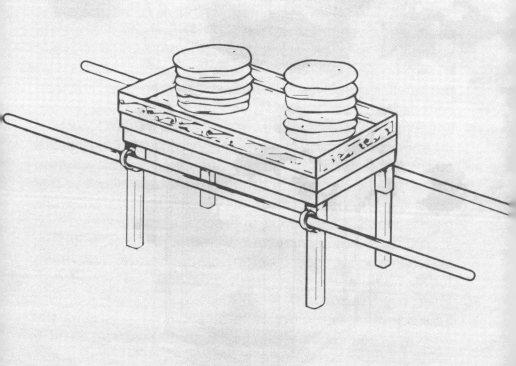

13 | The Table of Showbread

In the story of the girl in the room with the stream of visitors, the principal activity in which those visitors engaged was eating the bread that was on the table. In the actual Sanctuary, this bread was called the Showbread (or Shewbread), and was to be continually placed before the Lord on a specifically designed table. The only people allowed to eat of this bread were the priests, and they were only to eat of it after it had been set before the presence of God for a week, and then only in the Holy Place itself. Each Sabbath, fresh bread was placed on the table and the old loaves were removed. In many cultures, bread is a basic staple; without it and other staple foods, the necessary nutrition for health and life is lacking. Keeping with this idea, bread becomes a symbol of those basic things we need to repeat daily in order to maintain a healthy and vibrant existence.

Jesus says, *"I am the bread of life"* (John 6:48). He is here saying that He is the nourishment for our lives. He is the staple we need to eat daily in order to live a full life. Eating this bread represents our devotional time: it is the time we give to seeking God, in order to gain a deeper revelation of His character. Suffering a lack of physical bread makes the body get weaker and eventually die. So too, having a lack of Jesus daily causes our spiritual bodies to become enfeebled and the soul to die. It may seem like living a Christless life is not a big deal – especially when things appear exciting, fun and full of adventure. The thing is; we cannot see the death of the soul until it is too late!

In the dream, the girl in that room actually gave her visitors the bread on her table. For Our Girl, she gave most of her time to maintaining a close communication with That Boy. If we place ourselves in their shoes, the time we should spend getting to know God is very often spent getting to know other people instead. That Boy became everything to Our Girl, while God barely got a look. Similarly, the visitors to the girl in the room simply walked in, and she willingly gave them her time and attention from fear of having them walk out on her. But once they had taken their fill, they walked out anyway, leaving her with nothing to show for the time she had spent.

So many of us have given up so much without the slightest protest. We have kept silent, and allowed that silence to eat away at our consciences, while letting others consume the time we should have spent with God. Just like Our Girl and that girl in the room, we have nothing to show for the time spent with these individuals – at least nothing lasting or positive. Rarely does the thought enter our minds that we are spiritually starving ourselves into a silence that will last for eternity. It is time to take our time back: it's time to take God's time back! Let's set up regular 'meal' times so we can spend meaningful moments in the Word, with the same dedication we take to making sure we get our fill of physical food.

For those of us who have not been careful with our time in the past, and recognize an existing spiritual starvation, we can take heart. Here is a promise that we can be renewed:

"I will be as the dew unto Israel: he shall grow as the lily, and cast forth his roots as Lebanon." (Hosea 14:5, KJV)

The dew comes faithfully every morning and evening to refresh the earth. It waters the ground, ensuring a continual source of strength and life to creation, which then blossoms, producing things of beauty like the lily. We too can become as beautiful as a lily if we allow God to water us each morning and evening with His Word. As God fills us every day we will stop hungering and thirsting for things that only bring us temporal fulfillment. Instead, we will enjoy the beauty that will develop in our characters, and as Hosea says, we will *"cast forth [our] roots as Lebanon."* The trees of the Forest of Lebanon were used extensively in times past to build temples, palaces and fortresses. *"They plant their roots deep among the rocks of the mountains and boldly stand in defiance of the tempest...Above all other trees the cedar of Lebanon is distinguished for its strength, its firmness [and] its undecaying vigor."*[1] With consecrated effort and the Holy Spirit's power, we can spread our roots wide in the firm foundation of God's Word and display the same strength, firmness and vigor that characterizes those magnificent trees.

For many of us, spending this kind of time seems too hard. Let's look at another story about a father and son, only this time they were walking along a beach. The young son was picking up shells as they walked, and was thoroughly enjoying looking at all their varied colors and shapes. Soon the young boy had accumulated quite a collection, and was very proud of himself. As they walked, the father spotted a starfish a little way off, and pointed it out to his son. The boy's face lit up with excitement and the father said, "Go and get the starfish, son." So the son ran off a little way towards it, but then stopped. He paused for a short while then ran back to his father – without the starfish. The father was puzzled and asked, "Son, what happened? Why didn't you get the starfish?" The son looked forlorn as he said, "I just couldn't get the starfish, Daddy." The father sent him to try again...this time the son got a little closer, but once more paused for a moment and returned to his father without the creature. The father was getting a little worried, thinking his son might be showing signs of timidity. So, after giving the boy a short pep talk, he sent him once again to get the starfish. The son was determined this time; he ran all the way to the sea star and stood right over it. But yet again, he paused and seemed to think for a while, eventually returning to his father, for the third time, without the starfish. The father asked in disbelief, "Son, what happened? Don't you want the starfish?" The little boy looked up at his father with tears in his eyes and replied, "Yes, I want the starfish, Daddy. But I couldn't pick it up because my hands are so full of shells."

Many of us share the little boy's dilemma. We have become so content with the things we have picked up along the way in life, that when we come to something better we simply cannot reach out and grasp it. We are so filled with these other things that even our desire for the new – more desirable, and more exciting promises – cannot motivate us to get rid of the old to make space. Our time is already occupied, and we find no space for anything else, even personal devotion time with God. The truth is we are missing out on the big things: we are missing out on the starfish because we are refusing to let go of our shells. However, if we want something bigger and better, we must release some of what we are holding onto, especially things that make us comfortable. We need to take a chance, and step into the unknown, trusting that if we put God first He will be faithful, giving us something better than that which we are afraid to give up.

What if instead of waking up half an hour before we had to leave the house, we were to get up just five minutes earlier to study the Bible for a few moments? If we already spend a little time in devotion, can we be radical and extend it further? That extra time in bed may seem so necessary, but remember, the death of the soul is a gradual yet continual process. If you have never done it, or have fallen out of doing it, starting a devotional habit will be a gradual process, too. Just as there is no quick fix to physical malnutrition, there is no quick fix to spiritual starvation, either. Starting with a time allocation that is realistic and one we will maintain is the best way to begin our spiritual regeneration. From this solid foundation, we can then build a stronger, healthier temple where spending time with God on a regular basis becomes a natural habit.

The habit of spending time reading God's word begins with a decision; a choice that leads to action. As that action is repeated over and over again, it becomes a habit. Hard as it may seem for many of us, having regular devotions can become a habit hard to give up, because the results from that time with God will become so incredibly transformative that we won't want to begin our day any other way. Our godly habits form our character, and fit us for eternity. Our character, in turn, determines our suitability for heaven. Many of us are aiming for heaven while neglecting our time here on earth, time specifically given us to develop the character that will be our passport and ticket to the eternal Kingdom. We simply cannot neglect our responsibilities for the time we have today, for tomorrow is not promised to us!

"All flesh is as grass, and all the glory of man as the flower of the grass. The grass withers, and its flower falls away, but the word of the LORD endures forever." (1 Peter 1:24-25) If we want characters that will last for eternity, we need to spend time in God's Word, and build our characters from this foundation. Every material aspect of who we are or will become will wither and fade away. The only part of us that will last is that which has been fed and filled with the Word of the Lord, which "endures forever".

Let us choose to let go of our shells and pick up our starfish. God has promised us so much more than the things we are afraid to let go.

"For I know the plans I have for you,' declares the LORD, 'plans to prosper you and not to harm you, plans to give you hope and a future." (Jeremiah 29:11, NIV)

God's thoughts toward us are bigger and beyond anything we can imagine for ourselves. When we spend time with Him, there is no telling what He will reveal to us, where otherwise we would have limited ourselves to our own ideas. Since we have a Friend who thinks big on our behalf, we can be certain that spending moments with Him won't be a waste of time. So often, after that time we spend in the morning, God spends the rest of the day showing us His love – giving us even more reason to keep going back to His Word for more!

14 | Talking Longer

Mistake Number 5 - Doubting Previous Conviction

When God gives us an exit from a situation, we should take it without question. We should not look back like Lot's wife, but rather flee, just like Joseph did from Potiphar's wife: even if it means we have to leave our dignity behind. The mistake of doubting previous conviction began with Our Girl maintaining close communication with That Boy, and the results led to greater mistakes. Instead of fleeing with all her might, Our Girl crawled away at a snail's pace and kept looking back, hoping against hope that That Boy would catch up with her. She left because her conscience said she had to leave, but she looked back because, in reality, her heart was still where he was. Thus began the hope that things could be worked out with That Boy.

The condition of their spiritual lives left them both in different places with neither of them able to find happiness or God. That Boy had various questions and spiritual issues he couldn't, or wouldn't deal with, which left him discontented, always needing to be entertained and distracted by other things. Our Girl was very strict with what she believed was right and wrong without really understanding why, and this left her frustrated and spiritually restless. That Boy was a wanderer, Our Girl was a seeker, but the bottom line was that neither of them knew where they were going.

The 'break-up' lasted a couple of months. Just long enough for Our Girl to forget what had made her break it off in the first place, and for enough to be said to make her feel like it was her fault. It was also just short enough for those feelings of attraction to remain as strong as ever. Time can actually be dangerous if certain things are left open... Through their continued contact they regularly ended up discussing feelings and the possibilities of the future. For Our Girl this was frustrating, because That Boy would always say one thing on the phone, but then later, in person, he would do something completely different. On the phone, when it was just the two of them, he would say the most charming things, but when he was around his friends or in public he would be completely different, even shutting her out, so he looked like he was in control and she was the silly girl just hanging around.

For Our Girl, this two-faced behavior was extremely hurtful and undermined her hopes for trying to give their relationship another go. She was never sure where they stood because she could never rely on what That Boy had said to her during their conversations. His behavior should have served as a warning to her; this is something we should be aware of, too. Does the person we are with, or are interested in, treat us the same in public as in private? Are they different on the telephone, or via messaging to when we see them in person? If the answer is 'yes,' we have some serious thinking to do. It is likely that deep down, there are real problems that these 'alternative realities' are allowing him or her to hide behind. It is so easy to transform ourselves into perfect people online, but who are we face-to-face? By living out the most exciting and confident parts of our lives virtually, we can find the reality of life boring in comparison, leaving us too insecure to show vulnerability or be truthful about who we really are.

If we consistently live separate lives in the virtual world of social media to how we are in reality, we rob ourselves of the time to figure out who we really are. Often it is very difficult to have authentic spiritual experiences because we struggle with the foundational invitation made by God to 'come as we are'. If all we know about ourselves is who we can be online or by text, we will never feel adequate or be able to come to God with our real selves. Yet again, the enemy succeeds in keeping us isolated from a God who loves us more than we can comprehend. When we spend most of our time shaping our virtual identities, the reality of life will force us into a constant fight to make ourselves look better – often at the expense of the feelings of others. This was the situation that Our Girl found herself in with That Boy. She was in love with the virtual boy and desperately wanted him to make an appearance in her day-to-day reality. She knew deep down being hurt like this wasn't good, but she had invested so much time in talking with him that the 'potential' of what could be was too strong in her mind to be ignored. She wanted him and he wanted to keep her; they were both in it for themselves without the tiniest understanding of what it really meant to be together.

1 Corinthians 13:5 says that love *"is not self-seeking"* (NIV). In other words, love isn't about itself, it is all about its object or recipient. Our Girl and That Boy had much to learn about what it really meant to love. One day, after That Boy had 'switched' on her in public again, something inside her snapped, and she told herself enough was enough. And this time she really meant it...or so she thought.

She didn't call him and resolved to put him out of her mind. She wrote:

> "Well he phoned me at the end of that week to catch up and I was talking to him like he was just any old friend. I didn't carry on in any way and was actually quite off-handish. He noticed this and he said that we need to talk. As far as I was concerned I was done talking to him or expecting to talk because whenever we decided to talk, he'd avoid me and we'd never get anywhere. So the conversation ended with me saying yeah, he can let me know when he arrives, and then we'll chat. I was totally not fussed in my tone and that was it. However about 10 minutes later he phones back and was kinda silent on the other end so I told him to speak his mind. He said or rather asked me if I'd given up on us 'cause he feels like I don't care anymore. Well I was like, "Duh...what am I supposed to do especially after how he was the last time we met when we were supposed to 'talk'?" I said I figured after that last time we were over because nothing had been discussed as agreed, so I was accepting that we would just have to leave things. Believe me...I was so fed up of getting things sorted in my mind, deciding what I wanted, getting my hopes up, only to be let down and getting even more hurt. This tone and resolve of mine must have shocked him because usually I was the one pushing for things and making the effort.
>
> Well he just let go of everything and just poured out

everything that was on his mind and apologized for his behavior. He got a bit frustrated at one point whilst trying to tell me how he felt and he just said it. He said, "I love you."

My goodness I was shocked but not in a bad way. All I wanted to do was tell him that I loved him too but since that last time we met and my week of resolving, I couldn't...my emotions just weren't there to deal with it. He told me that "for the first time in 5 months I know what it is that I want, I've made up my mind." And I was like, "Oh my days, you wait until I've made up my mind and resolved to leave things before you tell me you want to make a go of it again!!" My head was a mess, I didn't know what to do but all I did know was that even though my heart was saying 'Go for it, tell him how you feel,' my mind had been seriously resolved to a point that I couldn't ignore. This was a serious discussion that was not to be rushed into. Conflicts of the mind and heart must always be dealt with thoroughly and objectively because ignoring one completely isn't good. Ignoring the mind leads to rash impulsive decisions that lack wisdom and can lead to pain. Ignoring the heart can lead to a life ruled solely by laws that don't allow for flexibility and hinder you from living a little and can definitely lead to pain and lack of love.

So he told me not to rush things, to think things through properly and I was like yeah, I will and we agreed to talk in a few days when he came to visit."

For the first time in all of Our Girl's entries since the start of her dealings with That Boy, she finally shows a small ray of wisdom. After a whole period of continued let-downs she had finally seen sense and decided to let him go. She truly meant what she said. She had concluded it was not sensible or reasonable for her to continue pursuing That Boy. She had been broken down and made to look like a fool far too long. She was so resolved in her mind that when she heard him say that epic three-word sentence, all she felt was an empty whisper of, 'I love you too but it's too late'. Our Girl should have taken greater care to listen to that whisper. In all honesty she had not prayed properly in so long that she was unable to discern the Holy Spirit's voice as He pleaded with her heart.

The heart is a precious thing; it is a crime to put it through such destructive situations. We do ourselves no favors by trying to save something we know is not right. If Our Girl had stuck with her resolve at that time and had trusted that life would get better, her story would have been so different.

Are you in a place in any way resembling that of Our Girl? Are you trapped by an idea of love that never seems to make it into your reality?

Little did Our Girl know then that her pain was just beginning. Her resolve wasn't strong enough because once again she was relying on her own strength; she didn't think she could bring God into her mess. It had been so long since she had really spent time talking with God in prayer that it was the easiest thing for the enemy to convince her with his usual trick: "You've gone too far, you're on your own now."

What a lie!

"It is Satan's work to fill men's hearts with doubt. He leads them to look upon God as a stern judge. He tempts them to sin, and then to regard themselves as too vile to approach their heavenly Father or to excite His pity. The Lord understands all this. Jesus assures His disciples of God's sympathy for them in their needs and weaknesses. Not a sigh is breathed, not a pain felt, not a grief pierces the soul, but the throb vibrates to the Father's heart."[1]

But instead of turning to the Source of real Love who would have sympathized, comforted and directed her, Our Girl relied on herself, and her heart won out in the end. That Boy had told her he loved her; what was she supposed to do? Even before they met up, she had already decided she would go back to him…but she convinced herself she was still considering things and was being 'sensible' with her supposed caution. She went right back to mistake number two, denying the reality of the situation all over again. Repeating this mistake in turn led to a repeat cycle of all the subsequent mistakes, but with much greater consequences.

Doubting her previous convictions was a huge error. Conviction for good comes when we finally allow the Holy Spirit to have a foothold in our lives. That's all He needs: the smallest token of permission, the tiniest glimmer of a soul searching for truth, and He is right there to meet the need saying, *"I will never leave thee, nor forsake thee"* (Hebrews 13:5, KJV). And as another writer puts it, *"The Holy Spirit never leaves unassisted the soul who is looking unto Jesus."*[2] In that last entry, Our Girl showed a small glimmer of the Holy Spirit's working in her: but because her mind was not focused on Christ and was instead centered on That Boy, she failed to actually benefit from the help available to her.

Despite allowing the Holy Spirit access into her life, there wasn't enough scope for Him to truly work on her behalf, because there was not enough room in her heart for Him. Instead, she had chosen to give virtually the entire space over to her feelings for That Boy.

At a later time, looking back, Our Girl wondered why God had allowed her to go so far down the wrong path. It was only later still she came to understand that by thinking this of God, she was claiming He had a duty to coerce her into obedience; that somehow He had failed in His duty of care. In actual fact it was her desires that caused her to walk away of her own accord. Isn't it ironic that when we are determined to do our own thing, we think it is such a good idea, but when we go wrong, we blame God for allowing us to do it? Even when we know God has said 'no' to whatever situation we want to get into, isn't it often the case that we still go ahead and do that very thing anyway? For many of us the likely answer is yes, because in those moments of decision our selfish desires outweigh God's voice speaking to our hearts; our feelings hold more weight with us than (even divine) wisdom. It is the love of our own desires that keeps us away from God's love and influence. We are the ones who have run away from Him, yet we wonder where He has gone when we end up in dead-end situations, alone and in pain!

God doesn't force His will on us. He has created us with freedom of choice and simply asks us to choose His way of love and protection. Our Girl's previous conviction didn't stand a chance because she wouldn't let it have sway. She gave no time to that still small voice that had said it was too late. She didn't even bother to pray about her upcoming meet up with That Boy. She had already made up her mind what she was going to do.

So after meeting up and talking, That Boy and Our Girl got back together...

15 | The Altar of Incense

The dimensions for this altar were given in Exodus 30:1-9. It was approximately half a meter wide and long, was overlaid with pure gold, and was placed in front of the veil separating the Holy Place from the Most Holy Place. On this altar the High Priest would burn sweet incense each morning and evening so the smell would rise up continually throughout the day and night. The position of the Altar of Incense in front of the veil meant the sweet vapor would not only rise up and fill the Holy Place but it would also waft over the veil into the Most Holy Place. As such, no strange or unauthorized incense was to be burnt on the altar, neither were any burnt sacrifices to be offered up on it. It was reserved only for the continual burning of sweet incense, for which God Himself had given the recipe.

So what do the altar and incense represent for us in our own lives? Here is a clue to the answer:

"Then another angel, having a golden censer, came and stood at the altar. He was given much incense, that he should offer it with the prayers of all the saints upon the golden altar which was before the throne. And the smoke of the incense, with the prayers of the saints, ascended before God from the angel's hand." (Revelation 8:3,4)

In the holy place of our own lives, the incense we are to offer up is our prayers. The incense the priests offered up before God was administered both morning and evening; so we can use this example as the basic model for our own prayer life. This specific time allocation of morning and evening falls beautifully in line with our daily devotion with Christ (remember the Table of Showbread), which Hosea describes as the morning and evening dew (Hosea 14:5). So our daily devotions and our prayer life work together harmoniously. The interesting point about both the bread and the incense is that they remained continually before God all day. The continual aspect of our devotion contributes to its lasting effect on our daily spiritual growth. Thus in the context of the Altar of Incense, it is written:

"Aaron shall burn on it sweet incense every morning; when he tends the lamps, he shall burn incense on it. And when Aaron lights the lamps at twilight, he shall burn incense on it, a perpetual incense before the LORD throughout your generations." (Exodus 30:7,8)

Similarly, our prayers ought to ascend perpetually throughout the day. But how does this work? How are we to have our incense of prayer continually ascending before God?

Prayer is essentially a discussion of our thoughts, ideas and questions with a Friend. The only method of getting our thoughts across to someone is to actually communicate with them. Prayer is like that: it is simply a way to speak with and confide in God, to share with Him what's on our hearts. Often we see prayer as something we should do or must do, but we can easily miss the real relationship God wants to build with us through prayer. It's not a chore to speak with a friend or someone we love. Why not? Because we know them, value their opinions and have learned to cherish their input in our lives. Similarly with God; He desires this same level of conversational relationship with each and every one of us.

Many of us worry about exactly how we should come to God to begin building such a relationship. We struggle with our feelings of inadequacy, and feel unable to approach Him when we are in need. For those of us who wrestle with this, we have the promise and hope of Romans 8:26:

"Likewise the Spirit also helps in our weaknesses. For we do not know what we should pray for as we ought, but the Spirit Himself makes intercession for us with groanings which cannot be uttered."

We have no reason to wonder what we should say to God: we have a Helper in all things, Who is waiting close by to aid us in our prayers and thoughts. The Holy Spirit works in our hearts as we allow Him access, through spending time in God's Word. He shows us that we are sons and daughters of God; that we belong to God and are loved and have a place with Him (Romans 8:14-16). If we are children of God, that means we can talk with Him freely and openly. It is every parent's desire for their children to feel confident and trustful enough to talk to them about anything on their hearts. God as our Heavenly Parent feels no differently. For this reason Paul says in 1 Thessalonians 5:16-18:

"Rejoice always, pray without ceasing, in everything give thanks; for this is the will of God in Christ Jesus for you."

It is God's desire for us to be in continual communion with Him. It's how He intended things to be, so we could always have a connection to the Source of our strength and happiness. This connection, described in John as branches (us) connected to the True Vine (Christ), is our lifeline: prayer is our lifeline, and prayer is simply sharing your thoughts, feelings and questions with One who is always ready to listen.

This call for us to have our incense of prayer going up before God continually does not mean we must spend the entire day on our knees praying. Rather, it means that as we go through our day, we should take God with us on that journey. Take Him on the bus or in the car to school, to college or university. Take Him to lunch, to the gym, to the store, to our friend's house and back home again. We do this by having our thoughts in the right place and on the right things, and it helps if we are around the right people, who support us in spiritual things. God is there for us at all times, no matter what; so why not check in and say 'hi' from time to time? When our colleagues walk in and out of the office, or if we see friends on campus multiple times a day, we smile every time we see them, don't we? It's not like we need to be on the phone with them all day to keep a connection going; we simply have little points of contact with a smile, a word or a thought.

The process is no different with God. It's easy to have the person we love on our minds continually throughout the day, because we have such a devoted interest in them. In the same way, by having a devoted interest in including God in our day to day activities and decisions, our thoughts will naturally become like incense going up before God continually as we seek His will in all that we do. The Psalmist wrote, *"Let my prayer be set before You as incense, the lifting up of my hands as the evening sacrifice"* (Psalm 141:2). The role played by the Altar of Incense in the Holy Place is an indication that prayer must feature strongly in our lives. Jesus' life was completely founded upon His prayer life. His constant communication with the Father was His lifeline in a world that did not know Him, and sought only to bring Him harm. Even as He hung on the cross, dying to save each and every one of us, His prayer was, *"Father, forgive them, for they do not know what they do."* (Luke 23:34.) Such was His love for us that He gave all to make a way for us to be with Him for eternity. This same Jesus wants to talk to us, and has shown by example how we can live a victorious life for God.

We can see that having good thought connections to God through prayer has many benefits. Conversely, we can understand the effects of having negative thoughts running through our minds and neglecting to communicate with God.

"Then the LORD saw that the wickedness of man was great in the earth, and that every intent of the thoughts of his heart was only evil continually." (Genesis 6:5).

If the condition of the people before the flood was so bad they had to be destroyed, we can see how having thoughts that are "evil continually" leads to both physical and spiritual destruction. The verdict of the Flood tells us there must have been a better option for the antediluvians to have adopted as their thought processes. The reason they focused on evil continually was because their actions and lifestyles promoted these thoughts. In Luke 6:45 Jesus explains why this is the case:

"A good man out of the good treasure of his heart brings

forth good; and an evil man out of the evil treasure of his heart brings forth evil. For out of the abundance of the heart his mouth speaks."

If we become involved with the wrong people and engage ourselves in destructive lifestyles, the thoughts of our minds and the words of our mouths will naturally run continually on bad or negative things. It is very difficult to lift yourself out of dark thoughts and feelings when surrounded by things promoting that state of mind. It's so important in situations like this to do whatever you can to get some breathing space, in a safe place away from your usual environment. To give yourself permission to be still, to think and to allow God to move into your situation. He longs to lift us up out of the black holes we find ourselves in, often with no idea of our own how to get out. Some of these situations cannot be figured out on our own; at such times seeking help from a trained counsellor can aid us in clearing some headspace, so we can begin to pray again or even start to pray for the first time.

Our Girl slowly lost her desire for spiritual things as her lifestyle degenerated to one where she simply did what she wanted. She gave no time to prayer because all her time was given to thinking things through on her own. This self-dependence caused her to become mentally and emotionally unavailable to spiritual things. Self separates us from a God who wants us to talk to Him without ceasing.

For many of us, prayer has become a difficult thing to get our heads around, especially where guilt over mistakes is involved. It is so natural to want to avoid conversation with someone if we know we have gone against his or her wishes. For these same reasons we feel we cannot come to God and talk to Him. This was a huge problem for Our Girl, because she felt God would be angry, and didn't want to face the shame or rebuke she thought would come as a result. How sad it is that we so often feel like this! Christ himself promises:

"And I will do whatever you ask in my name, so that the Father may be glorified in the Son. You may ask me for anything in my name, and I will do it." (John 14:13,14, NIV)

All we have to do is ask. Prayer is simply conversation. We can all talk...why is it that we have such a problem talking to God? Especially when His invitation is for us to talk to Him about everything?

Many of us have considered John 14:13-14, and have prayed, only to find that God didn't answer. Naturally this experience will affect our confidence in asking for something else. When this happed to Our Girl, she figured she was either too worthless for God to help, or He hadn't heard her because she had gone so far away from Him. Another thought was that perhaps she just wasn't praying right: that her 'formula' was wrong. How was she to know that none of these responses fit with the character of God? She had never taken the time to get to know Him. She didn't know He hears everything we say when we cry out to Him, or that there is no 'formula' for us to follow to get our prayers heard. If God says He will do whatever we ask of Him in Jesus' name, we must consider then, that there may be a difference between our prayers being heard and those prayers being answered. If God is indeed good, faithful, merciful and a Keeper of promises as spoken about in the Bible, and if He indeed wants good things for us and for us to be happy (as He says in Jeremiah 29:11, *"For I know the thoughts that I think toward you, says the LORD, thoughts of peace* and not of evil, to give you a future and a hope,") then surely our prayers should have been answered? Especially since He says, *"You may ask me for anything in my name, and I will do it."*?

So how is it that so many of us are plagued by unanswered prayers?

Does God lie?

The transcript of God's character is found in Exodus 20, in the Ten Commandments. Verse 16 says, *"You shall not bear false witness against your neighbor,"* or as the Contemporary English Version (CEV) says, *"Do not tell lies about others."* If we are commanded not to lie, would it be wise for God Himself to lie, and make void His own words? If that were the case there would be no sense in following Him – a God who imposes rules He Himself cannot follow. It is written:

"Thus God, determining to show more abundantly to the heirs of promise the immutability of His counsel, confirmed it by an oath, that by two immutable things, in which it is impossible for God to lie, we might have strong consolation, who have fled for refuge to lay hold of the hope set before us." (Hebrews 6:17-18)

Basically, God cannot lie, and because of this we can trust Him. There are very few things God cannot do, but lying is one of them...another is He does not change. We can be certain that the God of the Israelites, and Moses and Adam and Eve, is the *"same yesterday, today, and forever"* (Hebrews 13:8). So, because God does not lie and He does not change, we can have absolute confidence that we can take hold of His promises and know what He has said will come true.

The problem, then, if we feel we have unanswered prayers, is it leaves us with only one option: the discrepancy must be with us.

When God said in John 14:13 that we could ask Him for anything and He would do it, were there any provisos or conditions to His promise? Christ says, *"I will do whatever you ask in my name, so that the* Father may be glorified *in the Son."*

When we pray, do we understand what it means to ask in Christ's name? So often the words "in Jesus' name we pray," roll out of our mouths as a phrase we feel must be said; the question is why? Could it be that praying in Jesus' name means understanding the character of the One who gave up all for us? In many cultures, and especially the Hebrew culture into which Jesus was born, a name was given as a definition and hope for the character of that child: a name would often define who that child would become. To pray in Jesus' name means the very things we ask for should be in line with *who Jesus is*: His character and Person. Do our requests have this in mind, or do we simply ask for whatever we want, regardless of the implication? Are the motives for our requests to bring glory to God, or are we simply out for personal gain? Are our requests self-motivated, or Christ-motivated?

Of course we are to come to God with any request or problem, but the condition of getting answered prayers is not based on what we ask for...it is based on our motives.

Christ says, *"I am the way, the truth and the life. No one comes to the Father except through me"* (John 14:6). This means there is no prayer formula or word order we must follow for our prayers to reach God...no, Christ says clearly that we need only ask in His name and He is the way to the Father. Christ Himself will bring our prayers before God: as it says in Romans, " Who is he who condemns? It is Christ who died, and furthermore is also risen, who is even at the right hand of God, who also makes intercession for us. Who shall separate us from the love of Christ?" (Rom 8:34-35). God's love has made every possible provision for our prayers to reach Him. He wants us to talk to Him and He in return is ready to talk to us.

God says, *"if My people who are called by My name will humble themselves, and pray and seek My face, and turn from their wicked ways, then I will hear from heaven, and will forgive their sin and heal their land. Now My eyes will be open and My ears attentive to prayer made in this place."* (2 Chronicles 7:14,15)

Alongside our motives for praying comes our attitude. Many times we ask for things out of the selfishness of our hearts. If we could see as God does, we would often recognize that the things we want will bring us nothing but harm. Often we approach God with an expectation of what we want rather than a desire to understand what He wants for us. We want a relationship we know is bad to work out anyway, so we pray for it to get better and try to 'christianize' our requests with scriptures like, *"It is not good that man should be alone"* (Genesis 2:18). We want that job with the large salary so we can live life, or even put money into ministry, without stopping to think that we should *"seek first the kingdom of God and His righteousness, and all these things shall be added to [us]"* (Matthew 6:33). We seek after and request so many things based on the desires of our own hearts, while more often than not we give no time to even consider what the will of God is for us. Perhaps there is a better way, one we cannot see with our finite minds and perspective. Yet when we don't receive things the first way that popped into our fallible minds, we are tempted to harbor thoughts that God doesn't care or even that He's not there.

When we go to our parents to ask for something, we learn from experience that there is a certain way to ask if we want to be heard. We ask with proper respect and give good reasons for our request. But we appreciate that even though we ask, our parents do not always give us what we ask for: we completely understand that our parents are under no obligation to grant things to us. Why then do we hold God under obligation simply because we ask Him for something? If our parents say 'no' to our request, does their refusal cause us to suddenly think they do not exist? So why, if God says no to our requests, would we think He is not there, either?

James 4:3 says, *"You ask and do not receive, because you ask amiss, that you may spend it on your pleasures."*

Some prayers go 'unanswered' only for a time, some prayers are answered in ways we do not expect or ask for, and still other prayers go unanswered because God sees that there will never be a good time for us to have the thing we have asked for. Our prayers do not go 'unanswered' because God hasn't heard. He hears every request and actually answers each one either with a yes, a no, or wait. The term 'unanswered' is just our way of saying we have not got the answer we want; in reality God has answered but we were unwilling to accept.

Think about it another way: through prayer, God fills our lives with everything we allow. God cannot fill our lives with things by force. That goes for the good and the bad. Both enter our lives through the choices we make and the quality of our choices depends largely on how much we have chosen to allow God into those decisions. We are actually in the driving seat. Maybe those requests we have that seem to go unanswered simply cannot be given to us, because our choices and character are not allowing it. Choices about where we live, who our friends are, what we do with our time, our job, the places we go, the foods we eat, the conversations we indulge in. Maybe we are waiting to meet our idea of 'The One,' or we could even be willing to wait for God's ideal for a partner, but all the while we are making decisions which keep us on a path not crossing that person's, or that unfit us to be with him or her? Or maybe at this point in life a partner would keep us away from God and His purposes, through us getting too comfortable, or would challenge us so much we would lose our relationship with Him altogether. Our Girl felt she had a reasonable complaint regarding 'unanswered prayers,' when in fact God had answered her multiple times, in many different ways, but she had missed it because He wasn't giving the answer she was looking for. She knew the kind of guy she wanted to be with, but her lifestyle and decision-making were not placing her in line with that ideal. So instead she tried to manipulate things to make That Boy fit her ideal, slowly drifting away from trust in God and ending up trusting to herself, instead.

Our Girl eventually realized deep down that she'd reduced

God to being simply a Giver, with herself the taker. He was handy to have in a tight spot. She recognized that she wasn't truly interested in knowing Him for who He is, she simply wanted the relationship for what she could get out of Him.

She later learned that the prayer conversation goes two ways: we need to take the time when we pray to wait for God's answer. When we ask someone to do something we usually hang around so we can hear his or her reply, right? Leaving early from prayer, without waiting for God's reply, leaves many of us upset and distrustful of the whole exercise when things do not turn out as we expect. Good relationships work because of good two-way communication.

God's voice is never clearer than in His Word, and each page is a conversation for us to take part in. We may not hear Him right away, but as we draw closer to Him through time in study and prayer, He will draw near to us (James 4:8), and very soon we will begin filtering out the noise of life and His voice will become clearer.

16 | The Veil

So we have almost made it through to the place of God's presence! So many of the day-to-day bustle and duties of the Sanctuary were performed in the places we have just walked through, which is the same for us in our lives today. Everything up to this point was designed to prepare us for closer relationship with God and being in His presence and also to be in closer and more holy communion with those around us including our spouse or future spouse. As we go behind the Altar of Incense on the way to the Most Holy Place, we come to a curtain called the Veil. This curtain is made from blue, purple and scarlet yarn and embroidered with cherubim. In order to get to the Most Holy Place from the Holy Place, we must first pass through the Veil (Exodus 26:31-33).

The purpose of the Veil was to prevent anyone from accidentally or irreverently entering into the Most Holy Place, which was where God's Presence resided above the Ark of the Covenant upon the Mercy Seat. Accidental entrance into the consuming presence of God could only result in one outcome: death. But why? If God wants to be close to us, but death comes from accidentally or irreverently entering His presence, how exactly does the veil protects us and how can we know when it's safe to pass through it? God's Presence is described as a *"consuming fire"* in Hebrews 12:29, which can leave the impression that

God is unapproachable. If we look closer in His word, we will discover that God longs for nothing more than to be close to us. Revelation 21:3 says, *"Behold, the tabernacle of God is with men, and He will dwell with them, and they shall be His people. God Himself will be with them and be their God."* The reason God asked Moses to build a Tabernacle for His presence was so He could dwell with his children closely and be a visible presence in their lives. So too with us, God longs to dwell in our hearts, and the closer we step to the Most Holy place, the deeper God wants to be in relationship and the more important become the decisions we make in this area of our lives.

The Bible tells us that God is *"of purer eyes than to behold evil, and cannot look on wickedness."* Habakkuk 1:13. This is the reason for the enemy constantly working to keep us locked away in our cycles of mistakes and sin. He wants us to keep doing the very things that will keep us separate from God. It is he who tries to convince us that God is an unapproachable and distant God Who expects the unachievable and exists only to punish. How often we have viewed God from this perspective and shied away from His presence! We see God as the One doing the separating and miss the consideration that perhaps it is we who are the problem, not God. Perhaps all along it has been Him trying to get close to us, but our actions have kept pushing Him further from us, causing separation.

Sin separates us from God. It is our wickedness that God cannot look upon. God's eyes desire to look upon the pure things of life and when looking upon us, He sees the beauty of His creation marred by a dreadful disease: SIN. Sin was the reason why Adam and Eve were expelled from the Garden of Eden and the gate was guarded or veiled by an angel with a sword of fire. Sin was the reason Moses was unable to look upon the face of God and was instead hidden or veiled in the cleft of the rock when God passed before him. Sin was why the High Priest could only enter into the Most Holy Place once a year and was prevented from accidentally entering that area by the veil. Sin is the disease that does the separating, and we are all suffering from it.

Instead of thinking of the Veil as being there to separate us because God cannot bear to be near us, let us look at the Veil as being there for our protection because God cannot bear for us to be hurt. Adam and Eve were expelled from the Garden for the protection of humanity so that they could not eat from the Tree of Life and make sin immortal. If this terminal disease were allowed to infect humanity for eternity, there would have been no option for a cure. Adam and Eve were veiled from the immediate presence of God to allow God to put in place His plan of Salvation. This veiling had a purpose for that phase of humanity's existence. If sin were immortal, it would have been impossible for Christ's death and resurrection to make amends for us and bring us back into reconciliation with God. The separation at that moment was for a deep purpose that made for a more lasting provision of love later on. We will get into this idea more as we go along.

God's presence is the exact polar opposite of sin and completely eradicates it upon contact. Therefore, Moses was hidden in the cleft of the rock for his own protection — it was so that the Glory of God's face would not kill him because of the sin that was present in his humanity. Thus for the same reason, the Priest came only once a year before the Presence of God in a manner that set him apart for that service. Sin cannot survive in the Presence of God. 1 Corinthians 13:7 says that love *"always protects"* and *"God is Love."* 1 John 4:8. If we continue to see God as a Person who seeks to separate Himself if we do something wrong, we will never understand the reality that it is God who is always trying to draw near to us. We have no need to be burdened by guilt and shame if we recognize that God longs to heal our mistakes and strengthen us to withstand the snares of the enemy.

Surely if God has said Himself *"Come to me, all you who are weary and burdened, and I will give you rest"*, then He cannot be a God Who wants us to keep away from Him. He also says, *"I have come that they may have life, and that they may have it more abundantly..."* (John 10:10), which shows His concern for the preservation of life, so naturally, He has put measures in place for our safety and protection.

He says to come.

Even more so when Christ died, the veil that was in the temple of Jerusalem was torn in two from top to bottom. This was a symbol that we are no longer to be separated from God by sin because Christ has conquered sin on our behalf, and through Him we might enter into the very presence of God and not be consumed. Christ is the key to all things, He is that doorway, that Veil for us and every single aspect of the message of the Sanctuary points to Him. *He is in everything* and it is through Christ that we are able to move into the Most Holy Place and closer intimacy with God.

The Hebrew word for veil is pôreketh (po-reh´-keth), which means, sacred screen and its function is defined by the word perek (peh´rek), which means to break apart with rigor or severity. We have already discussed the sacred screen application of the veil in the sanctuary being for our protection from having our sinful natures consumed in God's presence. Now let us look at what that veil is supposed to 'break apart' and keep separate in our personal lives within the context of relationships.

This veil was there to separate the Most Holy Place from the Holy Place where, for us, our spiritual family is permitted to enter. Bearing in mind that our spiritual family is there to play a part in the services of the Sanctuary, their ministry is limited to the Holy Place because only the High Priest was allowed to enter through the Veil, and he did that only once a year. This is key because it is important for us to realize there are things that our parents, family and friends cannot do for us for which we need a High Priest. There is a work to be done in our hearts that only One who has prepared themselves to undertake this responsibility of High Priest can do. This next step is one of true dedication and duty.

First and foremost, Christ is our High priest as it says in Hebrews 9:11; He came and sacrificed Himself and it is His own blood that He is using to make atonement for us to release us from the guilt and consequence of sin. We can only have this process completed on our behalf if we choose to allow Christ to be our representative. The High Priestly duties can only be performed in their truest sense in our own hearts today by Christ. The daily sacrifice that was made in the Tabernacle on the Altar of Burnt Sacrifice was important to atone for Israel's daily sins but it did not cleanse their record of sin completely. Those sins were merely transferred from the penitent worshipper to the sanctuary via their animal sacrifice. It was on the Day of

Atonement that happened once a year that the Sanctuary itself was cleansed of that year's build-up of sin offerings. The High Priest transferred these sins from the Sanctuary onto a scapegoat which was released into the wilderness, signifying that the sins of Israel were no longer held on record in the Sanctuary. This is a type of the same process happening in heaven for us today with Christ Himself standing as our high priest. Our daily devotions, prayer and repentance serve to cleanse our hearts from day to day sin but they do not serve to clear our records in heaven of the sins we have committed. Those sins are recorded as forgiven but they remain on file, as it were. It is Christ Himself who then takes that record of ours into the very presence of God the Father, covers them with His own blood and stands in our stead pleading on our behalf for our records to be blotted out of the books. He pleads for their complete removal, never to be held against us again. What an incredible display of love, devotion and duty! Similarly, this sacred responsibility was placed on anyone acting as High Priest in the earthly sanctuary, because their actions had to represent the special work that Christ was doing in the Sanctuary of Heaven in every way.

Now let's take these duties into the sphere of personal relationships. Ephesians 5:2 says, *"And walk in love, as Christ also has loved us and given Himself for us, an offering and a sacrifice to God for a sweet-smelling aroma"* and goes on to say in verse 23, *"For the husband is head of the wife, as also Christ is head of the church; and He is the Savior of the body."* Right here in his letter to the Ephesians, Paul explains the parallel of the role of Christ as Savior and the role of a husband. That same sacred responsibility is wrapped up in the role of a husband and that intimate relationship between a husband and wife is supposed to be a sphere in which the gospel is to be played out. The gospel is about relationship, reconciliation, understanding, sacrifice, service, devotion and passionate, determined love. Marriage is to be all of those things!! But that role of husband, like the ministration of the High Priest, only happened once a year at a specific time; in other words, it was a special event, it was not a day to day or common occurrence.

This is the why the Veil was and is of such pivotal importance to us today. The separation of the Veil ensured that the ordinances of the High Priest on the Day of Atonement remained special and separate from the day-to-day duties of the Tabernacle, and served to keep the Most Holy Place and the articles held in there in a most reverent and honored place because therein dwelt the very presence of God. Withholding the most intimate and sacred parts of ourselves and veiling them from the day-to-day habits and norms of life ensures that when the time is right, and on the appointed day, the special sacredness of union can happen in all its fullness without us being consumed. Notice what was said there. Without being consumed. Many times, just like Our Girl, we open up the most sacred parts of ourselves: our mental, spiritual and especially physical purity and enter into sexual or intimate relations at a time not appointed and not with someone consecrated by God to minister in that area of our lives, which is why so many of us are consumed with pain and guilt. Brokenness was never intended for this intimate part of life. Everything about how we operate our bodies should be about reconciliation, restoration and rejuvenation. Ladies, sexual intimacy is intended to be with one person only, the High Priest-Husband sent by God at the appointed day and time and with no other. Gentlemen, sexual intimacy is intended to be with one person only, the Church-Bride-Wife you are to give yourself for, at the appointed day and time only, that God permits you to enter into. If we do not set up our veils to ensure these appointments happen at the right time we leave ourselves open for anyone to "fall into" our Most Holy Place and that unholy invasion will lead you both to be consumed. What a tragedy to arrive at the place of finding real love and intimacy only for it to be hijacked by the enemy with a counterfeit idea of love to keep us from having the presence of God in our relationships. It doesn't have to be this way. If you are tired of seemingly endless cycles of poor relationships with all the wrong people, erect a veil. Do it now through prayer and consecration, and ask Christ to uphold that standard in your life. He is faithful. As it was mentioned earlier, separation for a time is for a deep purpose that makes for a more lasting provision of love later on. Even now if you find you have made mistakes, it is never too late to veil yourself. Christ will begin the healing process and will continue to work out the details of your heart and reveal to you His plan for your lasting enjoyment in the Most Holy Place of your life. He will show you what true love really is, what it looks like, how it acts and how to experience it freely.

17 | Where is God?

The next place in the Sanctuary after the Veil was the Most Holy Place or the Holy of Holies. This was the area where the Presence of God dwelt. It could be said that trying to "find" God was much more simple in Bible times when the Tabernacle was a physical place that the Children of Israel could visit while they sojourned in the wilderness. If you wanted to know where God was, you just had to look at the Tabernacle. Later, when the Temple was built in Jerusalem, it was filled with the Presence of God before the watching Israelites, through a visible and awe-inspiring manifestation by cloud and fire, at its dedication.

But what about for us today? Right now as we are processing 1 Corinthians 16:19-20, how does the Holy Spirit of God dwell in us? Where does He come from and where do we find Him to even have the dialogue of allowing Him to enter our hearts?

The very simple reality is this:
You find Him exactly where you are.
He's right here.

Just decide to give Him a try. Let go of any preconceived expectations or notions of the God we think we know, and commit to a journey of rediscovery; challenge God to show you who He is on His terms. Going at life on our own was never God's intention, which is why most of the time, life may just not make any sense, or we feel like we have a lack of purpose or direction. These frustrations lead to a great sense of fear. Fear of the future, fear of what seems to be the unknown, fear that we will never overcome the brokenness of our past. A life characterized by fear is no life at all.

Psalm 34:4 says, "*I sought the Lord, and He heard me, and delivered me from all my fears.*"

Seeking God is the way to overcoming our past. It is the only way to finding peace in our present and having hope and confidence for our future.

God promises to deliver us from all our fears; not just some, all.

The peace we seek is only possible when we let God in to address all of the fears that we have developed over the course of our lives. The first step is letting go of the idea that we can figure things out on our own and deciding to see what God can do. We simply have to decide to see it from God's perspective. It's about having an attitude that says, "*No matter what I think, I'm going to see what God thinks and let Him decide what is to be done.*" This kind of attitude requires faith. But what is faith and why do I need it in order to 'find God'?

When trying to develop a relationship with God, it's very easy to want to see something physical or to feel some deep emotional sign that something is working or changing in our lives. The thing is, we are so wired to respond to sight and senses that we are totally unprepared to see through the eyes of faith. I don't know about you, but Our Girl had huge issues whenever she heard the word faith. What does faith mean? Is it even a thing? More importantly, how do you get it? Sure, we've perhaps heard the Hebrews 11:1 definition that, *"Faith is the substance of things hoped for, the evidence of things not seen..."* We hear it in church all the time, and it has become one of those memorized and almost cliché texts that everyone knows but rarely takes the time to explain properly.

The first word Our Girl had a problem with when she read that passage was the word 'substance'. Having a very scientific thought process, this word caused her to think that faith must be something she should be able to hold and measure in physical terms. Some of the definitions given in The New Oxford American Dictionary Online for the word 'substance' are:

"The real physical matter of which a person or thing consists and which has a tangible, solid presence." "The quality of having a solid basis in reality or fact."[1]

The problem with these definitions when applied to the Hebrews 11:1 passage is that faith isn't exactly something you can go buy at the store or order an amount of from the Internet. Faith didn't exist anywhere Our Girl could see and because she definitely didn't have any, it wasn't even a reality for her. To her, faith was not tangible, it was not a 'solid presence' so her conclusion was, either the Bible was wrong, or her understanding was wrong.

As she had that phrase in her mind, "no matter what I think, I'm going to see what God thinks and let Him decide what is to be done", Our Girl resolved to accept that somewhere she must be missing the point. She decided to look further and think outside the box. Now, if we look up the meaning of the original Greek word or perhaps look in the footnotes of our Bibles, we discover that another word which can be used for 'substance' is '*confidence*'. This type of confidence is one that enables you to endure or face anything. This word 'confidence' was one Our Girl had a much better time in understanding. Every day she woke up, she had *confidence* that when she stood up, she would be able to walk; that when she went to the tap, water would come out; that when she inhaled, she would be able to breathe in oxygen, etc. Having confidence in something is knowing that that thing is going to be there, that it is going to happen and we know these things purely because in our experiences, they have always happened that way in the past. So yesterday, the tap worked just like it did the day before that, and the day before that, for as long as Our Girl could remember. Therefore, logically, based on the pattern of the past, the tap should work without a problem when she turned it on today. Essentially, she had faith that the tap was going to work.

Now, I'm sure many of us are thinking the tap may not work, a pipe could burst, etc., and that's exactly right. This confidence or faith that we can have is not a guarantee of a result when we go to the tap; it's not a foolproof theory that once the tap is turned there is a 100% guarantee that water will come out. No, our confidence is based on the track record we have seen from what has happened in the past.

We live our entire lives based on confidences in things. When we sit, we trust that the chair will support our weight; when we cross at a pedestrian crossing, we trust that the cars will honor the red light and not run us over;

we trust that when we throw a ball in the air, it will come back down to us. All of these things have happened so many times in the past that we have 'confidence' or 'faith' they will continue to happen in that same way now, and in the future. These confidences that we have developed have also allowed us to form the habit of expecting them to continue to happen just as they have been. So, being able to have faith in God is being confident that the things we hope for in the future will happen because past experiences with God have taught us that He always comes through for us and has never left or abandoned us.

Now, the second part of Hebrews 11:1 was just as much a problem for Our Girl. The text continues on to say, faith is *"the evidence of things not seen."* What? How can we have evidence of things we cannot see? Let's look again as some examples from life. Each time we breathe in, we have confidence that there will be a ready supply of oxygen for us to inhale. But can we see oxygen? Of course not. So, if we cannot see oxygen, what makes us so sure that when we breathe in, our body will respond to that intake of breath and not suffocate? That confidence, or that faith which makes us take that breath is based on the *evidence* we have that oxygen exists. That evidence comes from the fact that every time we have taken a breath in the past, our bodies have been sustained and we have continued to live. We cannot see oxygen, nor can we feel it, but we know it is there. The fact that we're still alive is compelling evidence for its existence.

Faith or confidence in God is rooted and grounded in past experiences of God's faithfulness which have proven to us that similar encounters should happen again and again if we keep God at the centre of our thoughts and actions. Our personal faith will be evidenced by our experiences with a very real God, Who, if we let Him, will delight to show us countless ways in which He has already blessed us and can bless us in the future.

So how do we even begin to have these 'experiences' with God if we have never had them before? How do begin the journey in the first place?

This is where getting into the stories of the Bible during our devotion time comes into play. The people in the Bible are not simply characters in a play or some story, they really existed and secular records can prove many of these things to us. The God who did wonderful things for them still exists. The promises that that God gave to those people back then, all came true. We have Noah and the ark where the promised rain certainly came. There was Joseph standing before Pharaoh and the seven years of plenty and famine came. There was Moses and his experience at the burning bush followed by the promised deliverance of Israel from captivity. During the Exodus, God parted the Red sea for Moses so the children of Israel could escape Pharaoh. Later He parted the waters of the Jordan for Joshua so the Israelites could cross over to conquer the Promised Land. There are so many stories we can study into. We have abundant evidence that God is a God of promise; He is a God of covenant. The conquering of Jericho is an incredible fulfillment of promise because it was in silent obedience that the victory was won. Isaiah 30:15 says,

"In returning and rest you shall be saved; in quietness and confidence shall be your strength."

In coming back to God and resting or staying with Him, we

are promised salvation and it is in 'quietness' or in remaining still and having faith in God's promises, that we will find strength to face our trials.

The ultimate promise that God gave was to eternally save us from our mistakes and to give us a way back to Him; to give us a way back from the separation that sin had caused when Adam and Eve fell in the Garden of Eden. That promise was fulfilled when Jesus Christ relinquished all of His glory in Heaven, came down to Earth and took on our broken humanity, becoming the perfect Sacrifice in our place. This is, in itself, the most compelling evidence of God's love; a wonderful evidence in which to ground our faith. That which God had promised way back in the Garden of Eden, He was faithful to bring to completion. If we look back, there is indeed so much evidence of God doing amazing things for His people. Since He was more than able to exercise His power in the past, we can have sufficient faith that because, *"Jesus Christ is the same yesterday, today, and forever"* (Hebrews 13:8), He is still more than able to do wonderful things for us today and even for our future.

Our Girl eventually took the time to look back and saw the wonderful things that God had already done for her even when she didn't want to have anything to do with Him. There were countless occasions where she could see God cared enough to step in and save her. She remembered how she used to faint in the bath when she was younger and that on one occasion when she had fainted falling face down into the water and nearly drowned, God sent her dad to drag her out just in time. Another time when she was climbing a mountain, she got separated from her group and found herself stuck on a ledge which was only a few inches wide with a sheer drop way down to some nasty looking rocks and stones. When she was sure she was about to fall off and die, God sent her brother to find her and pull her to safety. She remembered driving in the car with her sister and almost missing her exit on the motorway as she was in the fast lane. She remembered panicking and just changing lanes towards the exit without even looking and yet somehow, despite there being traffic, she found herself on the exit ramp with no recollection of having crossed the two other lanes. Our Girl was shocked to realize that she had experienced a real life miracle. Given the speed at which they were traveling, and the fact that there was quite heavy fast moving traffic in all the lanes, she and her sister could have ended up in a massive car accident. If we look back, it is often the brief or small things in life which are so easily forgotten that are sometimes the most consistent evidences of God's care and attention. It isn't always the case that there will be some major event to mark the miracles of God in our minds, so we must be sure to search through everything when looking for our evidence. Let's not forget to notice the little everyday things.

Our Girl remembered how at one of the lowest points of her life, she had become so tired of trying to fix all her problems and troubles that she finally decided to give up. She was crying uncontrollably because of her failure when she heard Someone say to her *"go to Psalm 34:6!"* She thought, *"Ha! Yeah right! Now I'm hearing voices and must truly be mad"*, and continued to cry even harder. However, this voice in her mind persisted and eventually, out of cynicism and despair, Our Girl turned to that passage just to convince herself she had finally lost the plot. It reads: *"This poor man cried, and the Lord heard him, and saved him out of all his troubles."*
She was speechless.

She began to cry even harder because it was then that she realized God was right there with her all along; He was just waiting for her to give up trying to do things her way. She didn't know that text at all, and yet it spoke the very words she needed to hear to save her from despair. She was totally blown away that God would choose to speak to her when she had pushed Him out of her life for so long. The beauty of God is that He looks at the heart and He knew that her despair was rooted in the fact that she just didn't know where to find Him or how to begin to rebuild a relationship with Him. She didn't know that it was God that she needed; she just cried out and God heard her. God will honor His promises because He is God. It is in His character to fulfill His Word. This is why taking a chance on God and having faith in Him isn't really taking a chance at all; it's actually a super logical thing to do. It may seem strange at first but as we get into the habit of turning to Him in all that we do, the habit formed makes it easier to feel relaxed when it comes to God. It will become second nature to have confidence that God will hear you when you call even if He doesn't speak to you in an audible voice, He always speaks to us through His Word. Given the many experiences recorded in the Bible, there will always be something that shares similar principles and processes with anything we may go through. Take a look at what God says in those situations back then in the Bible and we will find those same principles work out the best even for us today. When we allow God to speak instead of trying to do all of the talking and thinking on our own, we will build up a wealth of experiences and our faith will grow continually. For Our Girl, this experience became one of the greatest evidences in her life that God is real and really cares.

It is so easy for us to forget that God can do things for us even now...but He can. He is the Great "I AM", not the Great 'I was' or the Great 'I will be'...but the *I AM*. He is more than able to deliver you now. God says in Malachi 3:6, *"For I am the Lord, I do not change"*. He is never going to stop being in the business of saving people. He gave His life for every single one of us. Faith is simply having confidence in the evidence of this. This faith allows God to dwell in our hearts in our Most Holy Place and it is this faith that helps us to allow Him to stay there rather than allowing something or someone else to take that place. Faith is the key.

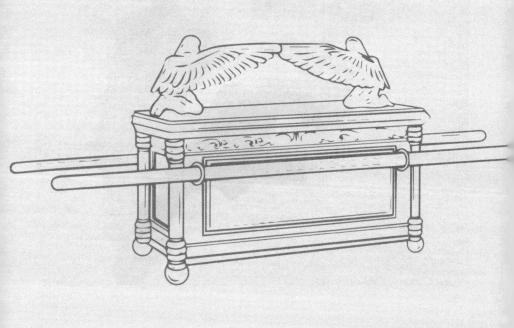

18 | The Most Holy Place

Restoration Zone 3

The Ark of the Covenant
The Most Holy place or the Holy of Holies was the compartment where the Ark of the Covenant was kept. The Ark was a rectangular box that was inlaid and covered with gold. It had two large cherubim positioned one at either end with their wings outstretched and in the middle of the two cherubim was the Mercy Seat. It was here, upon the Mercy Seat, that the Presence of God dwelt, making this the most sacred part of the entire Sanctuary. The Ark of the Covenant was at the very heart of the Sanctuary and it is the same in our temples. It is written: *"For thus says the High and Lofty One Who inhabits eternity, whose name is Holy: 'I dwell in the high and holy place, with him who has a contrite and humble spirit, to revive the spirit of the humble, and to revive the heart of the contrite ones."* Isaiah 57:15. The Holy of Holies, which contained the Ark, is our heart. It is here that God desires to dwell if we just humbly invite Him in. Our Creator longs to dwell within to us so we can be in constant connection to our source of life and vitality. What an incredible God! Our Girl never thought of God in this way but rather as a distant, aloof Ruler who would have no concern for her because she had turned away from Him. How often we also feel the same way! Yet, here is a picture of a God who wishes to occupy the most intimate part of us, and to keep us strong when facing life's trials

and temptations. Our God longs to be close to us; He is a personal God who is passionately desirous of a close and connected relationship with us. It is for this reason that it is so important for us to treat and protect our hearts like they are the dwelling place of God, because that's what they were built to be! This quality of relationship that God longs to demonstrate to us is what He wants us to have with the one He ordains and permits to enter the most intimate part of our hearts. The love that God reveals to us as we allow Him into our hearts is the same love He desires us to have with our spouse.

"Love is patient and kind; love does not envy or boast; it is not arrogant or rude. It does not insist on its own way; it is not irritable or resentful; it does not rejoice at wrongdoing, but rejoices with the truth. Love bears all things, believes all things, hopes all things, endures all things. Love never ends." 1 Corinthians 13:4-8 ESV.

The love God wishes for us to have with our spouse is to be devoted, selfless, faithful, consistent, passionate and enduring. God wants married couples to be in selfless pursuit of a consistent connection with each other in the same way He has demonstrated His love for us through the life, death and resurrection of Christ. This business of committing to love someone is a very sacred and intimate duty. This area of our lives is not one that should be open for anyone to gain admittance to because as we discussed earlier, those who enter the presence of God without permission are consumed. So much pain has been caused and experienced because we have too often allowed the wrong people admittance to this area. Pain can also result from admitting even the right person into this most intimate part of our lives by granting entrance at the wrong time. Temptation right on the verge of marriage is often the most difficult to resist just like it was for the children of Israel on the border to the Promised Land. We read in Numbers 25 how right on the verge of receiving everything God had promised to them, the children of Israel were induced into idol worship and sexual intimacy with the Moabites during one of their pagan festivals. Twenty-four thousand people died in the plague that went out among them as a consequence of their actions — they entered into intimate relations and were consumed. Sure, the children of Israel were still permitted to enter the promised land but what a scar was caused by such a great loss of life right on the verge of victory! It is even more important to guard your heart when on the verge of marriage so that you can enter that promised land without scars or regrets and can experience victory as God has promised. It may require the zeal of Phinehas to remain faithful to God's plan, but it is more than worth it! Zeal for God can only come from having spent time with Him and through knowing Him.

Christ Himself has said, *"Behold, I stand at the door and knock. If anyone hears My voice and opens the door, I will come in to him and dine with him, and he with Me."* Revelation 3:20. The 'stand' here is in the present tense. Clearly, God has not made any indication that He has changed His mind about dwelling with us. He is waiting for us even now to let Him in. Our hearts are built to be inhabited by God. There is a natural desire within each of us for a closeness that provides comfort and security, yet so often, we seek to fill that space that belongs to God with all manner of things such as guys, girls, work, sports, music, movies... whatever we can find. Sure enough, we feel like that girl in the room, where for a time, we are distracted from the draught of emptiness in our lives.

But for how long?

We are told, *"love never ends"*, 1 Corinthians 13:8 ESV. Or, as the NKJV puts it, *"love never fails."* So often, it is easier to fill our lives with work or service to others and we end up becoming slaves to the feelings we get when our efforts are recognized or when others appreciate our service. It often seems easier to build ourselves up from those feelings rather than spending time with a God Who knows our faults and weaknesses and shows us who we really are inside. It feels easier to work on things we can do with our hands rather than working on our characters. Being slaves to our work may bring rewards for a time but it can lead to extreme exhaustion or sickness which brings our work to an end. This, in turn, can leave us too burnt out for social interaction with others. Result? We feel alone and useless. So many things in our day-to-day lives become idols; it could be our friends, social events, sports, studying, homemaking, music, our boyfriend, girlfriend, children or spouses! An idol is anything that takes precedence of our time over time spent with God. Eventually these idols we set up in the hope of filling that God shaped space will break down or fail us in some way or other because they cannot replace real love.

There is only one thing that can fill us up and leave us fulfilled for eternity — the love of God.

Our Girl tried to fill the void in her heart with many of those things, only to find they did not last. As long as we are caught in the cycle of trying to find fulfillment in things that have no ability to fill, we will remain too caught up to have time to run to God and be filled once and for all. God's Presence is the last place Satan wants us to end up. That is why there is often so much warfare in the Courtyard and Holy Place areas of our lives. Satan doesn't want us to experience a Most Holy Place connection with God because when God is seated on the throne of our hearts, Satan is powerless to control us any longer. He knows that once we have had a taste of the Real Deal, we will no longer find satisfaction in the fake stuff he has on offer.

How many of us would willingly choose to walk to the other side of the world if we had the opportunity to fly there instead? Walking would take years and years and would be so dangerous and difficult. Chances are, we probably wouldn't make it. Similarly, we cannot make it to the Kingdom of Heaven with our own two feet; we would never make it in time. By His sacrifice, Jesus is offering us an all expenses paid, first class air ticket to the best destination the imagination could conceive of. Does it make sense to reject His offer and try to walk instead? The way to accept that ticket is to guard our hearts and have Christ dwelling in us to show us the way. He says, *"And behold, I am coming quickly, and My reward is with Me..."* Revelation 22:12

So what does God have in store for us in the Most Holy Place of our lives?

We read in Hebrews 9:4 that the Ark of the Covenant in the Mosaic Sanctuary had three things inside it. There was a golden pot of manna, the rod of Aaron that had budded, and the tablets of the covenant. Let's look at each one in turn.

Pot of Manna
The pot of manna was contained in the Ark to remind the children of Israel how God had provided for them in the

wilderness and had given them the food of angels to eat. If we have a roof over our heads, food to eat, clothes to wear and life in our veins, then our hearts too are in possession of the manna and provisions of heaven. Life is often a struggle and many of us will not have all of these provisions in abundance, yet, we are not to forget God's promises that He will never leave us nor forsake us (Hebrews 13:5) or the promise of Philippians 4:19: *"And my God shall supply all your need according to His riches in glory by Christ Jesus."* We have a wonderful God who longs to remain an ever present help to us. It is a great practice to get into the habit of keeping a prayer journal where you can write down your requests and log a date next to them as they are answered. This allows you to see that God is a very real help in all of the things that we come to Him about. Another way we can remind ourselves of our 'pot of manna' is by sitting down and writing out all of the things that you are thankful for every day. You will be surprised how much you have in spite of the challenges you may be facing with the things you feel you lack. It is a great activity to help us see just how many of our needs are met on a daily basis and it provides tangible evidence of God's faithfulness to His promises.

Exodus 16:31 tells us that manna itself tasted like wafers of honey, which was synonymous with God's promise to the Israelites to bring them to a land flowing with milk and honey. Each time the children of Israel tasted the manna from heaven, they were reminded of God's promise for their future. So too for us. The fact that God has worked for our good in the past and is still providing for us in the present is perfect evidence that He will keep His promises for our future.

"'For I know the plans I have for you,' declares the LORD,

'plans to prosper you and not to harm you, plans to give you hope and a future.'" Jeremiah 29:11 (NIV). King David was a man who experienced many highs and lows in his life and the psalms that he wrote about his relationship with God paint a wonderful picture of love and devotion. He wrote in Psalm 34:8: *"Oh, taste and see that the Lord is good; Blessed is the man who trusts in Him!"* Our pot of manna is our remembrance of what God has already done in our lives and it serves as a reminder that just like David, we can taste and see from our own experiences just how good God is and we can always trust in Him for everything.

Aaron's Rod
The rod of Aaron that had budded and blossomed was inside the Ark as proof that God alone has the ability to choose who He wishes to lead out in the service of His Sanctuary. God had chosen Aaron and his descendants specifically to minister before Him as High Priest and as representatives of the work and ministry of the Messiah. In Numbers 16, we read about the rebellion of Korah who was disgruntled at God's decision to appoint Aaron and his sons to this honored position and how he garnered support for his cause from many elders and the children of Israel. Korah represents the type of people who wish to enter our lives and have all the privileges and intimacies of a spouse with no knowledge of just how sacred that role is. These are the people, just like That Boy, who desire all the perks of intimacy without having a heart consecrated to conducting the service of our heart-temples in the way that God desires. These types like to love with their own version of love and to do things in the way they consider to be good in their own estimation. Their desires are not for service but for self glory and self gratification and just like the two men in that girl's room with the muddy boots on,

they are just out to take what they can before leaving our lives in a complete mess. Those who operate as 'Korahs' in this day and age don't always have the knowledge that their intentions and desires are self-centered and destructive. They are often operating from a very broken place in their own lives and are simply playing things out according to what they think is the right thing to do. That Boy truly thought he was loving Our Girl by his intimate attentions, but just like Korah, his disregard for the authority of God meant that his actions just led to a trail of destruction and pain.

In the account of Korah's rebellion, we see that God gave many opportunities for Korah to repent of his rebellion while he still had breath, but Korah and his associates persisted in trying to bully their way into the presence of God and were consumed along with those who refused to remove themselves from their vicinity. God does not see it as any small matter when we try to set up our own standards of love in place of those He has given and showed to us. God knows that any counterfeit image of love is a destructive lie which will only cause us pain. God longs to protect us from ever having to experience that kind of pain and so, just like in the aftermath of the rebellion of Korah, God will make it abundantly clear who He has chosen to minister in the most intimate part of your heart. God told Moses to instruct the people to present the staff or rod of each of their tribal leaders, 12 rods in all. Those rods were placed in the Presence of God in the Most Holy Place of the Tabernacle overnight and removed the following morning. Out of all the rods presented before God, each inscribed with a leader's name, only Aaron's rod blossomed and bore fruit, with the others remaining as lifeless sticks.

If we uphold God as the ruler of our heats and daily ask Him to sit on the seat of our hearts, He will make it abundantly clear who we should choose to have as our spouse. The people who come close to this area of our hearts should be laid out before God for a time through prayer and study of God's word. In time, God will cause the right person to blossom and bear fruit demonstrating the characteristics of God's love. So often we are seeking to love those who are nothing but lifeless sticks! We end up being the ones driving the relationship to keep it going, and things happen that are not in God's plan because it is we who are trying to inject life into the relationship rather than leaving all that to the Giver of Life.

God's intentions for us with Aaron's rod are twofold. Firstly, it helps us to discern without a doubt who God would have us unite ourselves with, and secondly, it acts as a standard that we should each aim for in our lives to show we are His chosen people. The blossoming of Aaron's rod demonstrated life, energy, vitality, and beauty and each of these are to be characteristics that we display through the way we live our lives. God's intentions for our lives are contrasted with Satan's intentions for us to remain as lifeless sticks. God has done everything in His power to protect our lives and give us a distinctive beauty and purity, but many of us have allowed ourselves to become trapped in cycles of compromise keeping us away from our true potential in Christ.

In Isaiah 27:3, God is speaking about us as His vineyard of people and He says:

> *"I, the LORD, keep it,*
> *I water it every moment;*
> *Lest any hurt it,*

I keep it night and day."

What a wonderful passage of God's tender love towards us! It is God's desire to nurture us to good physical and spiritual health. He waters us and provides protection through the instructions in His word to keep us from harm. Night and day is God's promise to us; He will not cease from His care of us.

The passage continues in Verses 5-6 saying:

*"'...let him take hold of My strength,
That he may make peace with Me;
And he shall make peace with Me.'
Those who come He shall cause to take root in Jacob;
Israel shall blossom and bud,
And fill the face of the world with fruit."*

Our instructions are to come and "take hold of (God's) strength"; strength is found in the Word of God. Through our time in the Word, we will find peace with God and the misconceptions that wrinkle our perception of Him will be smoothed out as the Holy Spirit brings us understanding of the true nature and character of God. The promise to those of us who will come to God is that we will find a foundation and root and we will blossom just as the rod of Aaron blossomed. Our life of vitality will be a great witness to the world of the love of the redeeming Saviour.

"Christ is represented by the vine that imparts the nourishment, the vitality, the life, the spirit, the power, that the branch can bear fruit, and then when affliction and disappointment come, you are to show altogether

a different character of fruit than the world. There is the evidence that you are connected with Jesus Christ, and that there is a power that sustains you in all your afflictions and disappointments and trials; and this power and this grace sweetens every affliction."[1]

The 10 Commandments
The final item in the Ark of the Covenant was the two tablets of stone upon which God had written the Ten Commandments. After He had written them, God instructed Moses to put this "Testimony" (the tablets) into the Ark where they were to remain (Exodus 25:16). When we apply this principle to ourselves, we can see that the Ark or the heart was made to store the Law of God. Before the Fall, it would have been so natural for us to have the Law in our hearts as we were perfectly made in the image of God. Man was created to be in complete harmony and close communication with God and yet look how sin has changed us to the point where we can only keep the Law of God in our hearts with His help! Satan is such a liar that he has convinced many of us that God's Law of Love is the disease and makes every part of us seek to eradicate it from our lives as something dangerous and to turn to sin instead. What deception! As we fall captive to this lie, the sin that is within us goes unchecked and like any untreated infection, it multiplies and multiplies until it fills our bodies with sickness and pain. We are all desperately in need of a cure. That cure comes through allowing Jesus into our lives. It is Christ who works in us and with us to eradicate the disease of sin that has crippled us for so long. This process will take time. Anyone who has had a cold will know that recovery is never instant, and if you do not spend the necessary time in bed recuperating, you will inevitably get sick again because your body is weak. So too, we must take

the time to heal fully from our past hurts and mistakes. We must take time to rest and take active steps to keep away from those things that brought us down in the first place. That may mean we cut ties with that boy or that girl, or that friend or that place. It could be that kind of music, that sort of entertainment, those social media platforms. Then, once those things have been removed from our bodies, Christ Himself remains within us as an Antibody to prevent that sin from ever returning and taking hold of us again. It is written:

"The mouth of the righteous speaks wisdom, And his tongue talks of justice. The law of his God is in his heart; none of his steps shall slide." Psalm 37:30-31

Having the Law of God within our heats is so vital to our survival; it is the only way we can keep upright instead of falling into sin's traps. This is our firm foundation upon which our feet will not slide or slip, allowing us to walk through life with confidence and peace as it is written: *"I run in the path of your commands, for you have set my heart free."* Psalm 119:32 (NIV). Those boundaries set in stone by the 10 Commandments are not there to clip our wings and restrict our lives like the enemy would have us believe. Rather, following the Law of God frees us from cycles of pain and destruction that most people don't even know they're trapped in, like That Boy who was trapped by the commonplace habits of going to nightclubs, dancing and drinking. Following God's law truly frees us from being slaves to popular opinion, pursuits and lifestyle habits, allowing us to run the race of life with energy, vitality and praise.

Our Girl was raised to know these freedoms and yet she

readily gave them up to be shackled. Why? Since she never took the time to know the reasons why these "rules" kept her free, Our Girl never learned to appreciate just how much of a blessing the Law of God is to those who embrace it. You cannot fully embrace what you do not understand, and she really didn't understand God's love for her at all.

19 | What is Love?

Mistake Number 6 - A Pivotal Misunderstanding

What exactly is love? Why do we seek after it? Why is it important to really understand it?

Why is it that we can be so sure we are in love with someone, and experience all the positive and euphoric sensations that we readily associate with being in love, only to be left with feelings of pain, rejection or betrayal later on down the line? Was it love that we were experiencing at the start of that new relationship, or something else? How could things have failed so spectacularly?

Chances are, we thought we were experiencing love because we had learnt what love should look like from the movies, supposed reality TV shows, the music industry, magazines and the general ideas upheld by the majority on social media platforms. What the world sells us as love and happiness is, in fact, a counterfeit which if properly defined is nothing other than lust and self gratification.

There is a very big difference between being in love with someone and being in lust with someone. You can tell which is which primarily by the actions that take place in those types of relationships, which are very clear and distinctive.

Lust is fueled by personal sexual desire and uses very little of the rational and decision making parts of the brain. We saw this with Our Girl when she met up with That Boy and he kissed her. As a result of the passion of that kiss, look at how quickly Our Girl's speechless fear of getting too deeply involved with him sexually, changed to feeling that what they were doing wasn't so bad after all, because what she experienced felt good. Her own personal lust and how her body felt easily overruled her conscience and all of the things she had been taught. Lust of itself has no governing principles and thus, incites a desire within us that cannot be satisfied. It leads us to become trapped in cycles of endless pleasure-seeking, always trying to feel more and more and going further and further to keep ourselves satisfied. Lust is a very powerful force within us along with attraction, and we would do well to beware of confusing these emotions with love.

Love *seeks* to *serve* regardless of the sacrifice; lust *seeks* to *receive* no matter the cost.

The prevailing sentiment right now is: *"do what feels good for you, don't worry about anyone else — you just do you."* Feelings and the gratification of them is paramount. So often, we are led to believe that love is primarily something we must feel rather than something we decide to do and become. "Love" these days is generally more to do with the need for sexual gratification and less to do with the desire for true, lasting connection and relationship. In a world where watching pornography is almost the norm, how do we navigate relationships where the likelihood is quite strong that the dictates and expectations of pornography will come into play? The pornography industry has done a thorough job of mis-educating individuals into believing that their feelings of sexual gratification equate to love. This couldn't be more wrong! Pornography numbs the mind and body from experiencing true love in the real sense of the phrase as well as destroying a person's ability to enjoy satisfying sexual intimacy when they do get married. As a result, marriages and families are falling apart because one or both individuals indulged in pornography and consequently, they miss out on all that God intended and designed us to experience. Pornography-fueled or not, how do we battle our desires and bring them into their rightful places under the control of the Holy Spirit?

We have been created in the image of God and, as such, are relational beings. We need and seek out the company and companionship of others and long for lasting, meaningful connection and attachments with those we become close to. In the marriage relationship, these desires find an expression in sexual intimacy alongside other cultivated activities like talking, studying together and socializing with close friends and family. However, the way we see relationships taking place in the media, the sexual intimacy and attraction aspect is played up the most, with very little time given to social interaction in other areas.

Physical interaction of any kind that leads to sexual desire outside of marriage is dangerous and not one of us can win against that kind of danger. It is written: *"Above all else, guard your heart, for everything you do flows from it."* Proverbs 4:23 (NIV). We are admonished to guard ourselves above everything else! That means guarding our hearts is of primary importance; more than school, college, work, social events and social interactions. Maintaining purity of heart must be our first thought as we go about our daily lives because from our hearts, everything else is gauged. Consequently we will measure everything by the condition of our hearts and the more negative experiences we encounter, the more clouded and damaged the lens through which we view the world will become. Is there is anything we are doing that is leading and tempting our minds and bodies into more intimate interaction before the appointed time? Are there any provisions we can make to keep ourselves accountable and away from avoidable temptation? I say avoidable temptation because the enemy will always construct ways to bring temptation upon us, but he will have a much harder time reaching us if we have hidden our hearts away from things he can easily use against us, like staying out late or entertaining late night calls, being alone with someone you are attracted to, logging onto certain websites or TV channels, etc. Remember the lessons from the Veil in chapter 16. Without that protective boundary that sets up standards for separation and distinction, the only resulting outcome was for those involved to be consumed and experience death. Heartbreak and betrayed love can very much leave you feeling like a part of you has died. It is not God's intention for us to experience this pain and so He longs to be the directional force in our journey to finding our life partners.

The wisest man who ever lived repeated the following charge three times: *"I charge you, O ye daughters of Jerusalem, by the roes, and by the hinds of the field, that ye stir not up, nor awake my love, till he please."* Song of Solomon 2:7 (KJV) The language is so pivotal here. We are admonished not to "stir up" or "awaken" matters of the heart until "he" i.e. God pleases. Have you ever shaken a can of soda and then opened it? What happens? Total explosion and mess right? It is the same with stirring up and then awakening love at the wrong time; the result is usually an explosion of feelings and a total regretful mess after. Also note the use of the words "my love": this isn't just any love, not the love the world would have us think is love; no, this is love as God intends it to be, the type of love that does everything as we see displayed in the life and sacrifice of Christ.

For some people, guarding the heart needs to begin much earlier, in the more simple interactions that, for all intents and purposes, seem innocent and harmless. For some individuals, sitting next to a person of the opposite sex with shoulders and arms pressed together is enough to lead the mind and body to desire more intimacy. For those of us who experience this, we should simply not sit like that; we should sit apart in order to guard our heart. For others, this may not be a problem but beware of falling into the trap of thinking, "if so-and-so can sit like that, then so can I..." No! We are all individual beings and God made us the way He did for a reason. We are each to guard our own heart and be mature enough to understand our individual personal limitations. By exercising self-control, we will be rewarded in ways that far exceed the rush of emotions that we get when we've stepped too far.

Although not everyone might understand this fact, holding hands is not a simple interaction. It is in fact a serious sign of ownership and can be a means of inciting deeper passions in the other person and in ourselves. However old-fashioned it may seem, know your limits and if you find your mind is being led further down the line to more intimate interactions, simply do not hold hands! ["Guard your heart".] Hugging is an interaction that naturally places two bodies in close proximity and has been designed to trigger deep emotional and psychological responses.

Studies have shown just how beneficial hugs can be to mental and physical health but the reasons why are precisely the reasons for ensuring any hugging interaction with someone of the opposite sex who is not your spouse is kept to a minimum and for a very short duration. When two bodies are connected in a hug for a prolonged length of time, the hormone oxytocin, which is also known as the "love" hormone, is released. In the realm of social interaction and getting to know someone of the opposite sex, we do not need any more of the "love hormone" than we naturally feel from simply being attracted to them. It's so easy to add fuel to the fire and more often than not, we end up getting burned. ["*Guard your heart*".] And to those who like kissing passionately and deeply outside of marriage, quite simply put, it is too dangerous for us to remain in control. Kissing in that way is designed to awaken the body sexually and eventually whatever self control you think you posses will run out and you will end up consumed by your passions and make mistakes that often lead to regrets. ["*Guard your heart*".] The fulfillment of love in its right context and at the right time with Christ at its centre, always leads to the building of wonderful memories and a deep sense of peace and contentment. Love should never lead to regret.

It is not just about *how* we do any of these things, but also about *when* and *why* we are doing them. Personal gratification and the desire to experience the feelings of love is a misguided and naïve approach to relationships. Love isn't merely a bunch of feelings; it is an actual state of mind. This is why clear, rational thinking is so necessary for all of life, but especially our romantic relationships in which our emotions play such a massive part!

Our Girl was far too caught up in her feelings after that first passionate kiss to realize the limitations of her ability to control them. She may have felt that she had no problem with holding hands and having That Boy's arm around her shoulders and the occasional light kiss, but her downfall came because of her choice to allow their light kiss to progress and open the door to that kiss That Boy gave her on their afternoon walk. She realized that the path of her decisions of compromise in seemingly small things set her up for huge mistakes in greater things.

Can you be honest with your heart in the same way? Maturity and wisdom come when we are able to see clearly what our limitations are and take steps to avoid our weaknesses.

Anything that leads us to sexual activity outside of marriage is the enemy's plan for our destruction and undoing. It has nothing to do with God withholding good things from us. It is written that God is the One *"who satisfies your desires with good things so that your youth is renewed like the eagle's"* (Psalm 103:5, NIV). God seeks to renew our lives and bring us enjoyment with timely gifts. It is the enemy who seeks for us to indulge in these gifts in ways and at times that bring us to ruin.

The Parable of the Lost Son is a perfect example of what can happen when we seek what has been promised to us before the appointed time. Luke 15:11-32 tells us the story of a son who was promised great wealth as an inheritance from his father. This son, wanting to live life his own way, decided to ask for his inheritance early. Having received it, he went off to enjoy his wealth. The problem was, this son did not consider the trials and issues that life would throw at him, and instead of treasuring his wealth to sustain him through the varying seasons of life, he squandered all he had on pleasure-seeking and self-gratification. He ended up losing everything and was left empty, broken and alone. He went to try and make a new life for himself in order to recover from his mistakes, only to realize he was worse off than even the lowest servant in his father's household. He went home and was received with open arms and was brought back into fellowship with his father.

How many of us have squandered our inheritance (in this context, our 'inheritance' means physical, mental and emotional purity) in following our own desires? Lasting happiness and joy have been promised to us, and yet so often, we seek to experience all of these promises before our allotted time. Just like the lost son, we end up empty, broken and alone. We try to fix our mistakes and shame by ourselves, only to realize that we were so much better off in our Father's house following His guidelines. We too can always come back to the Father and we will find Him waiting for us with open arms, but how much better it would be if we had never left home in the first place! The lost son in Luke 15 would never have that same inheritance again and so too, many of us will never have our innocence and purity again as they would have been had we not left home. But there is hope! In being welcomed back home we have the chance to be truly reconciled to our Father, allowing Him to restore within us a new inheritance — a renewed innocence and purity that does not whitewash the consequences of our actions but nevertheless enables us to experience the miracle of re-creation and new birth in Jesus.

We discussed earlier that the enemy will never content himself with the small area of our life that we have offered him. Rather, he wants our entire life and it wasn't long before Our Girl's previous convictions of what she deemed inappropriate came into question.

"Love... always protects..." (1 Corinthians 13:7, NIV)

In all of this, where was Our Girl protected by That Boy's love and where did she protect him by hers? A love that seeks its own pleasure has no concern for another's protection and being on the receiving end of that kind of love is not pleasant. We should each consider how we have loved in the past and even how we may be loving now. We need to think about how our actions can make others feel. I'm sure we can all find a time where we loved someone in a way that we thought was best and never took the time to think about the other person's individual needs. Often we think: *"this is the way I love and they had better get used to it."* The fact is, it is nothing if not cruel to think in such a way. Selfishness leads to loneliness. Protecting others and thinking of them is the only way that we can succeed in loving them in the way that they need. Clearly, neither That Boy nor Our Girl had a concept of a love that protects or guards from destruction.

So then, where do we go when the boundaries of propriety have been crossed? It is this simple: we either stop right where we are before more compromise happens or we can continue and face the consequent dangers of numbing the mind against what we know to be true.

"Truth does not depend on the unsettled and changing opinions of men. It was truth before it was believed. It will remain truth whether it is believed or not."
Carlyle B. Haynes.
Our Girl was too upset and hurt to know where to go or

what to do after she had ignored the truth for so long. Her previous gamble of not facing up to her situation and simply allowing it to continue meant she had set herself up to be cornered with no way of escape. And the consequences were humiliating.

We need to ask ourselves: are we in control of our lives, or are we being dictated to and simply following along as if both blind and dumb? Love protects even if the object of that love does not wish to be protected.

Our Girl should have allowed God to be the guard of her heart and innocence because only then would she have had the strength to withstand temptation. Instead, she allowed That Boy to take over. In her mind it just felt so nice not having to be the one trying to lead and direct their relationship all the time. After all this time, That Boy had finally taken the initiative, and he seemed so comfortable and content now that the relationship had become more physical. The truth was, everything Our Girl thought she was experiencing as love was in reality just the playing out of being in lust. She had known much about what was right and true but had never taken the time to learn the why behind those principles and that left her bereft of the strength she needed to stay true to those ideals when the temptation came. She hoped that her convictions would just go away and she could just learn to "enjoy" the direction their relationship had taken. She tried time and again to just numb her mind and emotions against how her heart was being affected. She learnt to "stuff" her emotions and hide how she was feeling; she made a habit of hiding behind a mask of enjoyment when really every interaction they had caused a little more of her to die inside. Because she chose to deny the truth, she lost who she was and what

WHAT IS LOVE?

was important to her and instead, submitted herself to be led by That Boy.

20 | Submission saved the World

Mistake Number 7 - A Misunderstanding of Roles

So what was the issue with Our Girl submitting to That Boy's leading? The issue was her misplaced understanding of roles. She had grown up seeing the male figures in her life being the ones leading and it seemed to work, so naturally she figured she should simply go along with That Boy's ideas of a fun time without question. The problem was that there were so many questions in her mind about everything they were doing. Even more confusion came when she encountered the passage in Ephesians about submission.

"Wives, submit to your own husbands, as to the Lord. For the husband is head of the wife, as also Christ is head of the church; and He is the Savior of the body." Ephesians 5:22-23

She understood the idea of submission as she was already doing that — so she thought — but the part about *"as to the Lord"*, she was not so clear on because she had got into the sad habit of not submitting her will to God. She had cleared her life of godly submission in favor of self indulgence. That left her with the misplaced notion that what she was doing was submission when in reality it was simply capitulation and compromise. She had nothing to stand up for and so she fell into the enemy's trap of just going with the flow of the ideas of those around her, and specifically, That Boy's ideas. The next line was even more of a conundrum for her: *"for the husband is the head of the wife, as also Christ is head of the church; and He is the Savior of the body."* She could see there was a connection with submission and the way Christ had given Himself for the church and she could see very clearly that there was nothing Christlike about their relationship. But for Our Girl, she was still trying to live the godly life in theory and simply couldn't accept that she had strayed so far from God and was not living up to His standards. She had elevated her own standards to the place where God's standards should have been and this led her to miss the fundamental distinctions that God places on our lives. She saw that she should submit herself to her husband, who she hoped would be That Boy, and simply hoped that all the other bits about Christ would fall into place in time by themselves. Deep down, she wanted a godly man to be the head of her home and to lead their family in worship and in Bible study and to use the precepts of the Bible to govern their home. She saw that the way God loved was consistent and reliable and fail-proof and she wanted that for her future marriage more than anything. Her biggest fear in life was ending up like her divorced parents, so she wanted the kind of love security that would make that outcome impossible. In her mind, she figured the best way of keeping the relationship going in the face of their lack of Christlike love, was to make sure that That Boy was happy and that they were not arguing or disagreeing about anything. The only way to keep that level of peace was to totally erase herself and her opinions from their relationship. She should just submit and let things be as they were and forget about her hopes and ideas for a Christ-centered love.

We have all been designed to fulfill certain roles that work together in harmony if everyone does their part. So many of the ideas that seem to have been prevailing in recent times reject the role designations that are outlined in the Bible and opt instead for the independent person approach with nobody feeling like they need to be accountable, subservient, or dependent on anyone else. Gender distinctions are being merged or clouded and the idea of gender based roles is seen as archaic, oppressive and an issue of equality. It is true that history documents many examples that demonstrate a poor use of power and unfair dominance of one sex over another and this has naturally led to feelings of resentment and a desire to break free and assert independence. The resulting actions are a reaction to a situation that God never intended to happen when He inspired the Ephesians 5 passage to be written. Godly roles and distinctions were put in place to protect and provide stability and to create a working harmony for humanity to thrive and be prosperous. It was never intended to give license to the miserable examples of male dominance and abuse to womankind that have been seen to develop over time. One sex was never meant to lord their power over the other with the other often being beaten into submission by force or by fear. Sadly, the word submission has garnered a poor reputation over time and is seen primarily as a word of weakness or a word denoting that someone is less than the person they submit to.

The truth is, however, that submission saved the world. Submission is a process of power and selfless action on behalf of another, which we can see from Christ's example of submission to His Father. In coming to Earth to die for us, Christ's self-sacrifice and willingness to yield to the will of His Father means that we can have a chance of a better life with Him - a life of real love and true devotion. Without

Christ's submission, we would all be lost, *"for the wages of sin, is death."* Romans 6:23.

Our Girl was so used to playing the role of leading their relationship in its beginning stages, that when That Boy finally stepped up and did the leading for once, she was too relieved initially to bother enough about the fact that he was leading her the wrong way!

Another truth is that submission is not a thoughtless act; it is a well-considered decision. Our Girl, however, didn't think; instead, she sat back and followed like a blind and dumb sheep. He, of course, felt more comfortable and content because he was finally able to lead and instigate plans for once. As things progressed, she became increasingly uncomfortable to the point where whenever they met, she couldn't enjoy herself and just relax in his company anymore. She was always on her guard to try and keep things away from the physical.

Whatever happened to innocence and enjoying the simple things in life? The truth was that their physical feelings had swiftly taken over the feelings they got from just being in each other's company and talking. As soon as the Pandora's box of physical interaction had been opened, they were simply not mature enough to understand that feelings like that have a limited life-span. They are strong, they are powerful and they can burn as hot as fire, but like any fire that has no fuel, the flames soon begin to splutter and die down to smoldering embers that eventually grow cold. There was no real fuel to their relationship anymore. They didn't talk like they used to; they were awkwardly polite around each other, whereas before they had been so much more relaxed and natural around each other. At least, it felt awkward to Our Girl because she knew that her conscience was being compromised. They were both struggling spiritually and God (and godliness) was nowhere to be found in their relationship. Instead, things settled on finding pleasure in the physical because there was nothing else.

All Our Girl could think about was how pointless their relationship had become — and how wrong. She just couldn't get away from the knowledge that she had been brought up with; she knew that love wasn't supposed to be like this. But eventually, she became so broken down with the pressure she felt to keep going further that she began to look at her blessed childhood as a negative. Why did she always have to be such a prude? Why couldn't she just get over herself and somehow forget about the things she knew were right and wrong? She just wanted peace but she was not willing to pay the price for real peace and pretty soon, she began to dismiss the cost of that peace. Having pushed her formerly naïve and innocent self into these new territories, she had no way of knowing if they could ever go back to how things were before they became physical or if she herself could ever get back to that innocence she had once had. Somehow, she doubted it.

Many of us like the way we feel when we are sexually active, but let's ask some questions. Does the sexual activity in which we are engaging really make us feel truly, deeply happy with a confident hope for the future? Do we feel secure in what we have done and are doing, or are there feelings of shame and regret and perhaps the wish that we had waited?

It is so important to be fully committed to our beliefs and knowing why we believe what we have chosen to believe.

We must either be hot or cold, for or against; because sitting on the fence and being lukewarm is the worst possible scenario. Fence-sitters who try to get the best of both worlds never get to truly enjoy the benefits of either. Christ says, *"...I would thou wert cold or hot, so then because thou art lukewarm, and neither cold nor hot, I will spew thee out of My mouth."* Revelation 3:15-16 (21st Century KJV)

The biggest issue here to God is people who think they can mix the spiritual world with the secular world. We cannot have both because by trying to have a bit of both, we actually prevent ourselves from truly experiencing either. The biggest shame of that is missing out on experiencing the lasting peace and fulfillment that has been promised in a life wholly given to God's leading. Lukewarm water is awful to drink! So too is a lukewarm life or a lukewarm relationship. There is very little fulfillment or contentment and nothing every feels truly satisfying. God desires that we embrace His ideas of relationships and how they should result in marriage rather than trying to go about them in our own ways.

The operative word in that last sentence is "trying" — because since we really were made to love God and be loved by Him, we can never truly succeed in finding happiness without Him. A life without Him can never be real happiness — not that real, deep down, completely assured and consistent joy that is not eroded by even the worst of life's circumstances. This kind of happiness can only come from knowing and loving God. Without God, we can get all sorts of happiness at many different levels. Some are surface levels of happiness more like a good sense of being entertained and occupied. This 'happiness' doesn't last and requires constant fueling to keep the emotional high going. Some types of secular happiness do seem to have much more depth, but a human heart that has said, 'no' to God can never experience the restoration of the heart that can only come through victory over sin (something that is impossible without God).

In His infinite love and mercy, the Lord knows and understands this carnal desire to find pleasure without Him and the constant energy required to maintain whatever pleasure-seeking treadmill we find ourselves running on. He knows that this is the plan of the enemy to distract us and wear us down. And so Jesus Christ gives us an alternative, saying:

"Come to Me all you who labor and are heavy laden, and I will give you rest. Take my yoke upon you and learn from Me, for I am gentle and lowly in heart, and you will find rest for your souls. For My yoke is easy and My burden is light." Matthew 11:28-30

We need to constantly remind ourselves that we have the option to carry either a) a heavy load, or b) a light load. In choosing our path wisely and following it completely, our load is always 'light.' Whatever happens, we have no need to worry ourselves into the ground. As the apostle Paul reminds us: *"being confident of this very thing, that He who has begun a good work in you [and in me] will complete it until the day of Jesus Christ."* Philippians 1:6

The sacrifice Christ made for us by submitting His will to the will of our Heavenly Father led to the greatest act of love the World could ever know. Christ's submission saved the world and by learning to emulate this same Christlike submission to the will of God in the way we conduct our lives and relationships, we will encounter the greatest experiences of love that we can ever partake in here on Earth with those we interact with and especially with our spouse.

Our Girl had failed to follow God completely and her conscience continually let her know about it. In all of her struggles with guilt, she realized her feelings were keeping her a prisoner and the knowledge that she was slowly losing herself made her miserable beyond belief. Too afraid of the consequences, Our Girl never told That Boy how she felt about what they were doing. She was lost and on a sure track to getting even more lost. As the psalmist wrote, *"Great peace have those who love Your law, And nothing causes them to stumble."* Psalm 119:165. Our Girl did not turn to God's Word where she would find peace, so she stumbled and fell time and again.

It is better to be a follower who fails every now and then, but gets up and gets back on track with God, than to be one who fails to follow Christ at all. Just allowing Him to pick us up after a failure will allow us to one day rise above that mistake and keep on going.

Our Girl never once thought that the Bible would be a good place for her to find real answers to her questions or remedies to heal her wounds. The Bible was the last place she thought she'd find love to fill that void that was in her heart. As a result of her spiritual isolation and hunger, she became disillusioned and her life felt empty. Her diary continues:

> **"I thought that by making him happy that I was making myself happy. WRONG... I gave up**

and compromised so many of my standards to accommodate his lifestyle and wants. Slowly I gave up on religion on a serious level. I still 'read' my Bible occasionally but most of the time I didn't bother. Then things got bad again when he started having problems in his life and instead of talking to me about it all, he would bottle it up and take it out on me. I put up with it for a good while thinking that it isn't his fault blah blah blah, that he had problems and I couldn't give up on him etc so I struggled on, trying to hold our relationship together... HECTIC TIMES.

At a particularly bad point when I had had enough I text him (because our conversations lasted barely 5 minutes at a struggle) and poured my heart out. He didn't even contact me. I told him he should contact me when he was ready to talk. Well he didn't call."

For the longest time, That Boy did not call and the final part of Our Girl broke. After that, there was nothing left to break. She had cried out to him with her last breath and he didn't have the decency to answer. Eventually, however,

"He called apologizing etc but I'd had enough. I decided to take my life back. There was no way that I was going to go running back to him as and when he'd sorted out his problems and was ready to have a relationship. I loved him too much to let him carry on hurting me and taking me for granted. I was such a fool. I gave too much of my heart too soon to the wrong person. For what I understood love to be then, I loved him with all my heart, completely utterly and truly. BIG MISTAKE. Sometimes God

offers you an exit route to avoid disaster and you should take it. I should have stuck to my resolve all those months ago. But no... me thinking that it was God's will, dived right back into the fire. I told him that I couldn't carry on like this and basically it ended.

I've NEVER felt so much pain in my life. Up until then I never believed in the pain of a "broken heart." But my goodness...it feels just how it sounds. I felt like someone had ripped my heart out and there was a literal empty, hollow, painful gap in my chest. So, so empty... just empty gosh. The pain. I don't like to be melodramatic but those weeks after we broke up, I actually felt like I was dying...no joke... the total and sheer hurt, pain and despair and feeling of loss were almost consuming. Don't give your heart away so early. You think you know it all and that parents "don't understand" but my goodness... they know what they're chatting about. I loved that boy and because of how deeply I felt for him, I know a part of me will always love him and that's another reason not to give your heart away freely 'cause a part of you will always remain with that person and when the time comes you have nothing decent left to give to your spouse."

That was the last entry Our Girl wrote at that time, and the memory of writing those words remained with her long after. She had no ability to feel anything except for the weight of emptiness. In her folly, Our Girl had made the most devastating sequence of mistakes she had ever made (or ever hoped to make) in her life. All this stress left her with no clue on where to go next. The greatest loss was the damage to her relationship with God, which she had sacrificed in the process of pursuing her own ideals. She didn't even dare go to Him after the reality of what she had done finally began to sink in, because she was so afraid of His rebuke.

Self-deception is such a dangerous thing. Many of us have asked (and still ask God) for a sign in these matters and wait for the smallest, silliest thing to happen and are so convinced that this must be the will of God — when in reality, we are simply seeking our own will and hoping that God agrees with us. We ask for signs instead of truly taking the time to get to know God intimately. This is a very naïve way to live as a Christian. If we really spend the time getting to know God, we will be able to know His voice and become much better at making the right decisions. Jesus once declared: *"This is an evil generation. It seeks a sign, and no sign will be given to it except the sign of Jonah the prophet. For as Jonah became a sign to the Ninevites, so also the Son of Man will be to this generation."* Luke 11:29-30. The signposts of examples that Christ has left us throughout His life are ones of surrender and submission to the will of God and spending time seeking God diligently in prayer and study.

Our Girl, however, kept away from anything that would require her to spend time in genuine spiritual activity. She wanted a 'quick-fix' solution to all her decision-making issues and was only interested in the fastest way to get whatever she wanted. So, because she thought God would drain her time, when she finally got free of That Boy, she *still* stayed away from Him! She was convinced that God was so angry and disgusted with her and figured she'd have to do so much to get back in His 'good books', that she could not imagine how long it would all take! She concluded she had gone too far to come back. So, she continued to struggle through life on her own making other (less epic) mistakes but by then, she didn't care because she figured she was too lost anyway.

How often we do this! Instead of seeing where we have gone wrong and stopping, we continue with reckless abandon so we don't have to face the consequences of our mistakes. Continuing only reinforces our error of judgment and our pride, showing all the more how much we need Jesus! Who we end up being and what we end up doing in public are often a result of the outworking of the secret hurts that we can't heal from.

Our Girl just kept on going with her hurt hidden away so much so that her public lifestyle changed drastically too. In order to convince herself that she was now the one in control of her life, she decided to go out and do all the things she said she would never do. In her mind, her 'control' came from deciding to go against all the things that were built into her conscience from her childhood. She simply purposed to prove a point to the world that she didn't care anymore. She thought that, 'not caring' was the only way to make the pain go away.

As a result of That Boy choosing his partying lifestyle above saving their relationship, Our Girl decided she was going to go and see what all the fuss was about and to see if it was all really worth it. Little did she know that by choosing to go down his path she was just manufacturing ways to feel close to him. She still wanted so much to understand why simply loving someone wasn't enough to result in a wonderful relationship. Our Girl was still trapped by That

Boy even when she was free of him.

This kind of behavior happens so often when the pain of a breakup hits. We unconsciously find ourselves doing things we never did before and liking things we didn't like previously. Many take up alternative lifestyles: over-eating, smoking, drinking, partying, sleeping around, listening to different kinds of music, etc., as a way of keeping a connection and numbing the pain. Many of the things we begin to do are often the very things that were an underlying irritation to us during the relationship. By doing these things we try very hard to convince ourselves that they are not really all that bad. Tragically, so many individuals exit relationships with the feeling that it was probably all their fault and if only they had done this or that differently, then perhaps things wouldn't have turned out the way they did.

That's how Our Girl felt and so she continued her cycle of mistakes and constant efforts to find happiness on her own. The truth was she felt so alone and was filling herself with anything to numb the pain. She was very much broken and she knew it.

So this is Our Girl's story, but what does it even matter?

It matters because Our Girl realized that time isn't always a healer, because it wasn't for her. It matters because just deciding to get over someone isn't always enough. It matters because without healing from past wounds, we are leaving ourselves open to more pain and no amount of covering it up can mask that hole that is there. It matters because if we don't face it now, we will face it again in the future.
We have all been hurt by many things in life and a lot of them

still remain ingrained in us on some level, though hidden away even beyond our own immediate notice. Perhaps if we look closely we will discover that certain wounds are actually still open, despite seemingly having healed on the surface. These could be anything from romantic relationships, bereavement, physical and/or emotional abuse, abandonment, or anything else we can think of that has caused us pain. Our Girl wasn't honest with herself. She tricked herself into thinking she was past her issues just because so much time had elapsed.

The reality was that she simply avoided facing the pain of loss, choosing to ignore it and bottle it up inside. She hoped that if she left it alone for long enough it would heal itself. But like we said at the beginning... why would it? We also said she tried to forget it... but how could she?

Without her realizing it at first, her guilt began to seep out and infect almost every other area of her life. In many cases, our emotional and physical wounds are best dealt with if we address our spiritual condition first, and begin a new journey of spiritual discovery (or even rediscovery). That was where God found Our Girl that night of The Dream and told her what she needed to hear to find the peace which had evaded her for so long.

21 | The Dream Part 2

As soon as Our Girl made her decision to let God take over, that room came to view in her mind once again and this time she took note of all that was in it. She saw clearly how each object in that room was supposed to have its place and serve a purpose and that by rearranging things according to her own standard, she had messed up the plan.

As she watched the man at the door, Our Girl soon realized that He was none other than Christ Himself. She continued to watch the scene before her as Christ waited at the door in pristine white robes, patiently holding that red bucket in His hand. Our Girl saw the girl in the room experience the same battle with the decision to let Him in that she had just experienced. She saw her looking at Christ amazed that anyone would knock and wait, when everyone previously had simply entered as they pleased. With sadness Our Girl saw the girl turn her back on Christ and continue to cry and hold herself in a hug of despair, apparently deciding that she was going to keep going on her own. Our Girl's heart sank and she willed for her to let Christ in to see what He had planned. The girl finally turned around to face Jesus and shrugged her shoulders and nodded for Him to come in, if that was what He wanted. Our Girl then saw Christ come into the room and close the door behind Him. He walked over to the girl and held her until she cried out her last tear and wiped her eyes. Then He Himself got on His hands and knees and began to clean up the mess on the floor using the contents of His red bucket while the girl stood quietly gazing at Him in deep gratitude. Our Girl realized that the girl she was watching was now responsible for keeping an eye on the door, while Christ's role was to clear, clean and purify the room. She saw the application: it was the blood that was shed by Jesus Christ on the cross that made it possible for that room to be cleaned. She felt so sorry that because of her, Christ would now have to stoop so low in her dirt, just to cover her sins and to save her. But as she watched, she saw that Christ was doing the work of cleaning up with a smile on His face. "What wondrous love is this?", Our Girl thought to herself.

Soon the room was clean and ordered, with everything in its rightful place. The fire had been stoked and fresh bread laid at the table and the room soon began to radiate a warming glow. Christ remained there with His arm around the girl to keep her company while she continued to wait and watch the closed door. This time she was waiting for a knock and Our Girl could see that as long as the girl kept Christ in the room of her heart, she would never again allow uninvited guests to enter. The room was clean, her heart was whole and on her face she wore a smile.

Some time passed and there came a knock at the door. The girl looked up at Jesus' face to see what He would say about the person knocking, and He shook His head in response. So she cracked open the door just wide enough to slip out a sign to whoever was knocking at her door. On that sign was written the message, "Do you not know that my body is the temple of the Holy Spirit who is in me, who I have from God, and I am not my own? For I was bought at a price; therefore I will glorify God in my body and in my spirit, which are God's." That message stated clearly that the girl was not available for any relationship that did not serve the purpose of glorifying God. It showed that she was done with her previous types of relationships that only boiled down to surface interactions and premature intimacies; she now knew her worth in Christ and was unwilling to compromise it again. Our Girl saw how the girl was completely sealed up with Christ and that having Him there made it so easy for her to know when a distraction from the enemy was knocking at her door.

A little more time passed and there came another knock at the door. The girl again looked up at Jesus and this time He smiled down at her. Our Girl was so intrigued to see what would happen next and watched with such anticipation as the girl opened the door. In walked a guy who had a little mud on his shoes, but as soon as he entered he immediately took them off and laid them neatly by the entrance. He looked at the girl and smiled at her but he didn't go near her, instead he walked straight over to Jesus and knelt down at His feet and waited. Jesus laid His hands on his shoulders, offered him a hand and lifted him up to stand beside Him then together they walked over to where the girl stood watching. Jesus placed the guy next to the girl and He stood close to them both holding them together.

As the scene passed from her mind's view, Our Girl lay there utterly humbled by God's love towards her. He cared! God actually cared so deeply that He had taken this time to reveal to her the condition of her heart and to show her a better way, a way that included a promise that meeting the 'right man' was possible with God residing in her heart. Words could not describe the feeling of peace that flooded Our Girl's heart that night after she decided to let God in. For so long she had failed to realize that all Christ needed was permission to enter. How incredible that the Great God of the Universe was waiting for her consent? Truly He had said: "Behold I stand at the door, and knock: if any man hear My voice, and open the door, I will come in to him, and will sup with him, and he with Me." Revelation 3:20 (KJV).

How long will we make Him wait before we answer and say yes?

God showed everything to Our Girl that night to bring about her healing. It was so simple, so plain, and once she made that decision to accept the help offered and let Christ in, a tide of peace just washed away her guilt and shame. Our Girl knew then that God had known everything about her guilty secrets all along and had now covered them with the blood of His Son, taking them away. She saw that it was possible for her to be made whole again. She realized for the first time just how much God loved her and how little those she had let into her life had really loved her. She saw that if she truly allowed God into her heart, He would fulfill the promise recorded by Ezekiel: "Then I will give them one heart, and I will put a new spirit within them, and take the stony heart out of their flesh, and give them a heart of flesh, that they may walk in My statutes and keep My judgments and do them; and they shall be My people, and I will be their God." Ezekiel 11:19-20.

From the moment she read this passage, Our Girl clung to it and decided to believe its truth. God showed her that she had nothing to do with the process of getting her life to blossom with freedom and vitality, it was all about what He was going to do for her. Looking at the text again we can see God says He will give us one heart —that is — a heart of unity... He will give us a new spirit, which is a new attitude or approach to life. He promises that He will take out our old stony heart that has become hardened through pain and guilt, and instead it is He who will come in and heal us and give us a new heart that is full of life. The next bit is so important for us to understand. God goes on to say that it is only then, AFTER He has done all of these things for us, that we will be able to follow His law and to keep His commandments. Isn't that incredible? That had been another major thing that had troubled Our Girl. She couldn't figure out how she could do right, especially after having done so much wrong already. She had thought she had to fix it all herself before she could come to God. Countless times we may have tried to 'fix' our problems and to stop doing the things we know we shouldn't be doing, only to find we can't. It seems we have got the whole process in the wrong order, hence the repeated failure to bring about real change. Change is a process and a process takes time. For the smaller things, the process may be instant, but for deeper and more difficult habits, there isn't a quick fix. We have to resolutely allow God to work these things out of our lives. Daily surrender gives Him permission to do this work consistently. Christ is waiting patiently to do this... "and they shall be my people, and I will be their God."

Christ places emphasis on the heart because He knows the heart is the very organ that physically keeps the body alive. But the heart in spiritual terms is linked seamlessly with our minds, thoughts and emotions working in harmony. Wrong thoughts or uncontrolled emotions lead the heart to experience pain and our lives to play out the result. The heart as our Most Holy Place is of paramount importance to our spiritual and physical well-being. It is for this reason that we are given the instruction:

"Above all else, guard your heart, for everything you do flows from it." Proverbs 4:23 (NIV)
The NKJV renders the translation:

"Keep your heart with all diligence, for out of it spring the issues of life."

Out of our physical heart, our lifeblood flows and so too out of our spiritual heart does our spiritual life flow. If our hearts are clean, so too will the rest of the areas of our bodies be clean. If we choose not to heal from our pain and guilt, this open wound in the heart will pump the infection throughout our lives causing other problem areas to develop. We are told to look after our hearts "with all diligence" meaning serious care must be taken when it comes to sharing the most personal part of ourselves with another. Too often we have experienced that out of bad situations, "the issues of life" spring in abundance. For Our Girl, most of her 'issues' came directly from her carelessness in sharing her heart and body with That Boy and sure enough, the issues didn't remain just in that area of her life. Bitterness and hurt have caused so many of us to blossom negative traits of character. We may have developed a nasty temper, and manners of speaking harshly to others. We may have become a disloyal or intolerant friend finding it impossible to really trust anyone, and becoming suspicious of everything. We may even have changed into a withdrawn and quiet shadow of our former selves riddled with fear and constantly seeking approval from others. Like Our Girl said at the beginning, her guilt over the years became the source of all of the crippling insecurities she began to develop in other areas of her life. She couldn't fix those insecurities until she allowed God in to heal the source of her 'issues'. Once He had begun His clear up, all of those other issues began to disappear on their own. Often we are trying to 'fix' something that isn't really the root of our issues but merely a fruit. Fruits blossom and change with the seasons and so too our issues will manifest themselves in so many ways that we can only be sure we are rid of them by allowing God to dig out the root.

Above ALL else, we are to guard our hearts. It is our primary duty to guard that door just like God has shown us with the girl in the room scenario. She was to keep an eye on the door as Jesus did the cleaning, and even after He had finished, it was still her task to keep watch with the support of Jesus remaining there with her in that room. We are never left alone to struggle with anything. God is there to help us every step of the way and when we have no strength to go on, God will carry us until we are strong enough to walk on our own again.

Crippling our ability to walk by keeping us from God is Satan's primary goal to keep us in bondage to him. Christ seeks to get us into good habits that will free us to be ourselves.

Satan's law binds and cripples... God's Law liberates, strengthens and blossoms a life of vitality where before there was just a lifeless stick.

Which will we choose?
Our Girl saw that the pain-free, guilt-free life she wanted really was available to her as a gift. The reality God showed her was that He had already made provision for her mess and His blood could wash away anything that she could have ever done, or anything that had been done to her.

The fact that Our Girl saw Christ remain in the room with the girl encouraged her to know that Christ promised to dwell within her own being. Because of His presence in her life, she could claim the assurance of Isaiah 60:13, where God says, "The glory of Lebanon shall come to you, the cypress, the pine, and the box tree together, to beautify the place of My sanctuary; and I will make the place of My feet glorious." Having Christ walking around in our sanctuaries is a sure promise of being filled with wonderful things and the beauty that comes from God's indwelling presence cannot be compared or replicated! The forest of Lebanon was a large forest full of evergreen trees and the bark of these trees was used extensively throughout Bible times for serious building projects — not least Solomon's temple! Each of our lives can be a place of life and vitality, evergreen with the blessings that God has promised to us all. All He says is "Come," and He will do the rest. It finally became clear to Our Girl that her life could again be useful.

With joy and contentment in her heart for the first time in years, Our Girl knew that everything was going to be ok and went to sleep at peace.

22 | The Epilogue

In light of our discussion, the most important thing we can do now is to stop and think about all that has been said. Just like in prayer, if we get up too quickly we will miss our answer. The same is true of this book. If we get to this point, read the last sentence and then put it down and walk away from it, we will miss the opportunity for our healing and restoration to become a reality; the quick exit will allow the enemy to convince us that our deliverance is just an idea. How many books do we have to read and how many sermons do we have to hear before we actually begin to do something about the state we are in? Our Girl had to ask herself the same question. She had read countless books and heard a lifetime of sermons and yet for most of her life, she had missed out on the truths that were always at her fingertips. She simply didn't take the time to really think about them. The promises of God can be made a reality in our lives in the same way they have been made real in countless others. We must make our decisions and claim the promises that Christ has given to us in His word now.

Christ says in Isaiah 61:1:

"The Spirit of the Lord GOD is upon Me,
Because the LORD has anointed Me
To preach good tidings to the poor;
He has sent Me to heal the brokenhearted,
To proclaim liberty to the captives,

EPILOGUE

And the opening of the prison to those who are bound,"

Christ came already! He has already fulfilled His mission of restoration for us. He came specifically because He knew that we would experience the pain of a broken heart, so He wanted to come and make a way to fix it. He knew that we would find ourselves prisoners to the endless cycles of mistakes that the enemy has trapped us in, so He came to set us free. He also knew that there would be circumstances in our lives where we would feel like we were chained in a prison, perhaps by our parents, guardians, relationship choices or bad experiences; and He came to open that door for us and show us what life is like with Him. Rest assured that what Jesus "opens no one can shut, and what he shuts no one can open." Revelation 3:7 (NIV).
Walk free.

God's sole purpose in sending His Son to die for us on a cross was to make a way for us to get back to Him, and to get back to our original state. Isaiah shows us that Christ's mission was to heal and to restore and it is 100% possible. Believe me!

As I sit here typing this to you I have the deep seated contentment that I am no longer that girl, or Our Girl, I am a contented woman, a well loved wife and a very busy mother. This relationship blueprint of the Sanctuary really does work. It guided me on a new path that eventually lead to my Mr Right knocking at my door. I found my promised healing and forgiveness and was filled to overflowing with gratitude and love for a God Who seeks us out and meets us where we are. Christ will not stop until He has achieved His mission for your life too. Verse 4 of Isaiah 61 promises that:

"They shall rebuild the old ruins, they shall raise up the former desolations, and they shall repair the ruined cities, the desolations of many generations."

Jesus really did come and bind up my wounds that night, although they were already so many years old. He has given me a new zeal for everything by giving me a new heart to experience life afresh. The love I have developed for Him through discovering who He really is by spending time at my altar of Showbread, by communicating with Him at my altar of Incense and through shining my light through talking to others has brought about the fulfillment of this promise in Isaiah. God is building up the ruined cities in my life and I have the confidence and assurance that my time of mourning is over, just as it can be for you. Together with Christ we can raise up the old desolations in our lives from our mistakes and the guilt they have left us with. The offer made to me, is the same offer made to you too — the opportunity is yours for the taking.

Time now is a healer because I have given God that time to work His love into my life. Will you do the same? Through the sanctuary message we can all have clean and protected bodies with practical instructions about maintaining a living temple for God.

This process is not an overnight fix, but it can be an overnight relief once we make the decision to stop and let Christ in to begin our clean-up. That clean-up will happen as quickly as we will allow it, and to keep clean is a daily exercise. Daily, we must minister in our courtyards to ensure we are encircled by the right people who will influence us for good and will encourage us to offer up acceptable sacrifices to God. Daily, we must work with our closer spiritual family to keep up the services in our Holy Place. Each day we must light our candlestick and share God's truth with others. We must remember to ensure the Showbread of our personal daily devotion is always before God, both morning and evening and we must not get tired of offering up our incense of prayer to God continually, for Christ Himself desires for us to come to Him in all things. The Most Holy place of our temples — the heart — must be protected by the Veil and only one who God has ordained to minister in that area, should be allowed admittance. Wait for that person; it will be worth it a hundred times over. Storing up the commandments of God in our hearts is the surest way of remaining on a path of purity and victory, a path which blossoms with strength and success.

These small things, if maintained, will work change that lasts for eternity. The final stage of our restoration will be when Jesus Christ comes to take us home with Him and we are changed for the final time — physically — into the likeness of God as it was in the beginning. The time that we have now is for us to transform our characters into God's image so that when He comes, He will recognize us as one of His own.

Let us choose life.

Let us choose to carry Christ's easy burden, for He says: *"My yoke is easy and my burden is light..."* This is our single duty — all we must do is carry the light of truth, which is the gospel; we can all share the truth with others for we each have a story to tell. Being on fire for Christ is far better than burning under the shame of guilt and pain. God has shown us the way out of our disasters to a path that will never lead us to live those cycles of mistakes again. Restoration is promised:

"Do not wait to feel that you are made whole. Believe His word, and it will be fulfilled. Put your will on the side of Christ. Will to serve Him, and in acting upon His word you will receive strength. Whatever may be the evil practice, the master passion which through long indulgence binds both soul and body, Christ is able and longs to deliver. He will impart life to the soul that is "dead in trespasses," Eph 2:1. He will set free the captive that is held by weakness and misfortune and the chains of sin." [1]

"I, even I, am He who blots out your transgressions for My own sake; and I will not remember your sins. Put Me in remembrance; Let us contend together; State your case, that you may be acquitted."
Isaiah 43:25-26.

Today, will you come to God and find the love and healing your heart longs for? No longer do our lives and stories need to be marred by insecurities and pain, we can be free and when Christ sets us free, we are free indeed. He asked me to write this story to you so you too can experience His healing. The time for your healing is now and God is saying to you as He did to me that night:

"My child, wake up."

Acknowledgements

Without the tender whisper of God's voice in that early morning wake up, this book would never have happened. So my first thanks, with deepest gratitude, is to my Heavenly Father Who took the time to reach out in such a special way to a girl who's heart was broken and who's mind needed healing. Thank you for desiring restoration for me and for giving me the instructions and words needed to share this message of hope with others.

Thank you to my incredible husband Clive. You are God's gift to me, the man of promise that God showed me would come. You are more than I could ever have hoped or dreamed for. Thank you for your love, support and encouragement.

Taneisha Messaoud, you are beyond words. I love you so much. Thank you for all of the four & five hour heart to hearts and for loving my children as your own.

Zippora Anson, you have been my soul sister from that first conversation we had that lasted for hours and hours even though we had only just met. You have been a priceless gift to me over the many years of our friendship and I'm so grateful to you for all the sound advice and spiritual lessons you have shared. You have been a such a consistent source of encouragement to me and I thank God for you.

Kia Chisholm you are such an incredible friend to me. I owe you so, so much. Thank you for understanding my heart and for sharing your insights with me in a way that has helped me to grow and become more confident as a person. You have given me so much strength in some of my darkest moments and I thank you for walking beside me through those times.

Cassandra Beccai, I knew from the moment I saw you that we needed to be friends! God worked it out for us to meet and discover a kindred spirit in one another. Thank you for the great conversations that helped me to keep writing in those early stages and thank you for sharing your heart with me in so many ways.

Tamara Muroiwa, your sensitive and Spirit-filled understanding of this project was clear from the start. Your discernment and advice have helped to make this book far better than it would otherwise have been and I will be forever grateful to you for joining me on this journey and for the many hours you have spent helping me to "preserve my voice" in the text and for making my mumblings coherent and ready for print.

Karin Dusabe you came on board so willingly at the 11th hour and helped to get this project completed in time for our deadline! Thank you for your hard work and for your comments that kept me encouraged and laughing during the editing process.

Thank you Kenneth Rivera and Ashley Bloom for all the

design help and amazing illustrations! You guys are awesome!

Mrs Gallant! You were the first person to make a real impression on my heart when we arrived in California and made yourself available if there was anything I needed. Thank you for reading through this book and making sure everything was readable and spelled correctly!

I'm so grateful to all my Weimar family for being the best support group we could hope for being away from all our family. You guys have been wonderful beyond words!

And finally, thank you dear Reader for getting to the end of this book! May God grant you more than your hearts desire as you commit yourself into His tender care.

Endnotes

Chapter 7

1   The Review and Herald, Jan. 31, 1907
2   White, Ellen G. Counsels on Stewardship p. 197
3   White, Ellen G. Maranatha p. 148.3

Chapter 9

1   White, Ellen G. Counsels to Physicians and Medical Students. PH 167 2.1

Chapter 11

1   Haskell, S.N The Cross and Its Shadow (Hagerstown: Review & Herald, 1914 p. 29)
2   See 2 Timothy 3:1-7, particularly verse 7.
3   See 2 Timothy 3:5.

Chapter 13

1   White, Ellen G. Patriarchs and Prophets 450.1

Chapter 14

1   White, Ellen G. Desire of Ages p. 356
2   Ibid p. 302

Chapter 17

1   (https://www.lexico.com/en/definition/substance)

Chapter 18

1   White, Ellen G. Reflecting Christ p.355

Epilogue

1   White, Ellen G. Desire of Ages 203